Queens of Power

Discover The Hidden Legends Of Muslim Female Rulers Who Shaped Islamic Empires

SARAH GULFRAZ

Copyright © 2025 Sarah Gulfraz

Sarah Gulfraz has asserted her right to be identified as the author of this Work in accordance with the Copyright, Designs and Patents Act 1988.

All rights reserved.

No portion of this book may be reproduced in any form, stored in a retrieval system, stored in a database, or published/transmitted in any form or by any means, electronic, mechanical, photocopying, recording or otherwise, without prior written permission of the publisher.

Dedication

~ Bismillah ~

May Allah (swt) accept our efforts and grant us success in this life and the next. Ameen.

In dedication to my loving family and all their support.

Contents

1. Introduction — 1
2. Asiya bint Muzahim: Wife of Pharaoh — 3
3. The Legacy of Razia Sultana — 11
4. Sultanah Taj ul-Alam Safiatuddin Syah of Aceh — 19
5. Nur Jahan: The Power behind the Mughal Throne — 26
6. Shajar al-Durr: The Queen of Egypt — 33
7. Amina of Zazzau: The Warrior Queen of Nigeria — 39
8. Arwa al-Sulayhi: The Queen of Yemen — 45
9. Zaynab Al-Nafzawiyyat: The Influential Consort — 57
10. Queen Aisha Al-Hurra: The Last Muslim Queen of Granada — 62
11. Rabia Balkhi: The First Persian Poetess — 70
12. Sultanah Safiyya: Power and Politics in the Ottoman Empire — 76
13. Queen of Sheba: Her Mighty Throne — 83
14. Conclusion — 89

Find Out More — 93

Chapter One

Introduction

A lady who adheres to Islam is known as a Muslim woman. Islam places a great value on women. A woman's role as a child, spouse, mother, sister, or in other capacities is highly valued and respected in the Quran and Sunnah. According to the Quran, Islam does not distinguish between men and women based on commitment or duty. Islamic teachings truly take into account, respect, and defend women's rights and place them in a respectable position based on the Quranic verses and the Prophet Muhammad's (PBUH) Hadiths.

Muslims believe the Quran is divine and its revelations are the ultimate authority. The second most authoritative source is hadith, the recorded sayings of the Prophet Muhammad (PBUH) that were gathered and documented in the ninth and tenth centuries, about two centuries after his passing.

Since Islam's birth, women have occupied political leadership roles in many Islamic countries and empires. Some were independent officials, while others were regents for spouses who were unable to govern or male successors who were too young to do so at the time.

Some proved to be brave military leaders, astute and capable administrators, or both; others were little different from their equally flawed, power-hungry male colleagues and planted the seeds for their own demise. There are numerous historical women in the Quran who, despite not being direct political leaders, altered the path of history and served as role models for future generations. There are several examples throughout history of these strong Muslim women influencing powerful men (or males in general) to alter their relationships, dynastic successions, and sociopolitical events.

From the early decades of Islam to the end of the seventeenth century, this book explores the lives of some of the most notable female rulers of Muslim caliphates, empires, and dynasties. This book will provide detailed information about the crucial roles played by Muslim women rulers in the history of Islam. Each chapter focuses on different influential figures, offering insights into their lives, achievements, and the lessons they impart. These queens and rulers not only held power but also influenced their respective regions' political, cultural, and social landscapes.

Their experiences show that numerous women have attained positions of authority and functioned as successful leaders throughout the religion's lengthy history. These women were respected, even feared, by their modern world counterparts and held in high regard by the people they ruled. A few notable rulers' lives and contributions are examined in a way that will serve as an example for future generations.

Their power and leadership demonstrate that, despite the strength of prevailing religious beliefs, certain regional cultures and political customs have produced results that contradict and weaken those beliefs. These women have had a lasting impact on their communities for thousands of years, sometimes altering the course of history and at other times having a major impact on important areas of life. In Muslim civilisation, remarkable women from many backgrounds and faiths collaborated with men to improve their communities.

This book focuses on women who have interacted with the current systems of authority and power, conquering personal and institutional barriers to become monarchs. Today's young women and men look up to them because of their inspirational tales, endearing personalities, and unwavering commitment to improving their surroundings.

Chapter Two

Asiya bint Muzahim: Wife of Pharaoh

Have you ever desired a closer relationship with Allah (SWT)? Develop your faith and practice only to encounter harsh criticism, probing questions, or worse? Have you ever felt compelled to give up something to follow your Islamic beliefs, even if it went against the wishes of your family, friends, or even your own spouse?

It's a lonely situation, however we can find inspiration in a role model who story has been preserved in the Quran: Asiya bint Muzahim. She is a woman who achieved unwavering faith, a loving and compassionate queen who recognised right from wrong in her culture despite being married to the most powerful rulers and living in extreme wealth.

She ultimately dared to stand up to her husband, the Pharaoh, and advocate for justice by stating her faith in Allah (SWT). She was a living example of faith, courage, and strength, serving as an enduring role model for generations to come.

Asiya in Islamic Tradition: A Symbol of Faith

One of the finest women in history is Asiya bint Muzahim (RA), sometimes referred to as Musa's (AS) adopted mother and the devout wife of the Pharaoh (Firaun). She was the spouse of one of the greatest villains in history, the Pharaoh. His immorality, godlessness, and haughtiness are well-known. As a result of her bravery and faith, Asiya (RA) is one of the four women who have been granted paradise and serves as an example for both men and women.

> *Ibn 'Abbas (RA) said: the Messenger (PBUH) drew four lines on the ground, then he said, "Do you know what this is?" We said, "Allah and His Messenger know best." The Messenger of Allah (PBUH) said: "The best of the women of Paradise are Khadijah bint Khuwaylid, Fatimah bint Muhammad, Asiya bint Muzahim (the wife of Pharaoh), and Maryam bint 'Imran – May Allah SWT be pleased with them." (Musnad Ahmad)*

Allah (SWT) uses her as an example to show believers that even a powerful oppressor and unbeliever's wife can convert to Islam. Allah (SWT) granted her Imaan despite the fact that her husband, the Pharaoh, detested the truth of Islam and persecuted believers day and night. Allah (SWT) has immortalised her because Asiya Bint Muzahim is mentioned in the Quran as the one who said the following prayer:

> *"My Lord, build for me near you a house in Paradise and save me from Pharaoh and his deeds and save me from the wrongdoing people." (Quran 66:11)*

Asiya (RA), the Queen of Egypt, was likely a member of the royal family, which was then known as "a family of gods." Yet, she must have been seeking the truth, and what Moses (Prophet Musa) (AS) brought resonated with her. Choosing to believe in the One True God, she willingly sacrificed the splendour, authority, and luxury of palace life. This act required immense bravery and sacrifice. In return, Allah (SWT) used her as an example for all believers: the recompense.

Life in Ancient Egypt: The Historical Context

Pharaoh, one of the greatest tyrants in history, insisted on being revered as a deity. He made monotheism and worshipping Allah (SWT) illegal and punishable by torture and death because he could not bear to see anyone worshipping anyone or anything but himself. "I am your Lord, Most High!" he demanded.

Egypt was a highly developed civilisation at the time; they constructed pyramids that are still standing tall today and were so precisely planned that they could be seen from above. Because of the Nile River, Egypt is blessed with excellent soils that support thriving crops and animals. Just think of what Firaun owned and how wealthy Egypt must have been!

The only people who still possessed some knowledge were the Bani Israil individuals. A long line of prophets had produced the noble dynasty known as the Bani Israil. Hazrat Ibrahim (AS) was the first, and Hazrat Ishaq (AS) was his second son. He had a son named Hazrat Yakub (AS) who went by the nickname Israil. A series of circumstances led to Hazrat Yusuf (AS), Hazrat Yakub's (AS) tenth son, becoming the monarch of Egypt. Therefore, he invited his father and eleven brothers to Egypt. The twelve tribes of Bani Israil were founded by their descendants.

They eventually strayed from Islam's actual teachings. Allah (SWT) consequently overcame them with shame and suffering. He brought them under the rule of the Pharaohs, among the most brutal rulers in history. They discovered that Allah's (SWT) favour was based on morality rather than ancestry. The Pharaoh enslaved them. However, he could not completely ignore the allure of knowledge and, despite her wishes, married Hazrat Asiya (RA), a woman from Bani Israil. Since everyone and everything in Egypt belonged to the Pharaoh, she had no way out.

Imagine a lady with access to wealth, power, and a position of prestige. Despite being married to someone who claims to be a god, she believes in the one real God. Not only is he delusional in his arrogance, but he is a harsh and vicious tyrant. Yet, her unwavering faith shines through, revealing its true beauty.

Asiya's Role in the Story of Moses(Musa (AS))

She is arguably most recognised for her role in the Prophet Musa (AS) narrative: She once noticed a box floating through the Nile River's currents while she and a few of her servants strolled along it. When she opened the package and saw baby Musa, she was enamoured with the child's beauty. It was evident at this stage of her life and marriage that she was unable to conceive; Pharaoh exploited this as a pretext to have children with other women, and Allah (SWT) confirmed that this was because Asiya (RA) was too good and pure to bear Pharaoh's kid.

> *She came back with that baby and pleaded with her husband, "(Here is) joy of the eye, for me and for you. Do not slay him. It may be that he will be of use to us, or we may adopt him as a son.' And they perceived not (what they were doing)." (Quran 28:9)*

She must have recognised the fact that the infant was an Israelite boy. Given that Pharaoh ordered the execution of all Israelite male infants, she was aware that the soldiers would murder him. At that time, Pharaoh had a worrisome dream in which he predicted that one of the boys would grow up and usurp his throne, so he ordered the execution of all infant boys born to the Children of Israel. The Pharaoh's army was meticulous and merciless. Once a child was born, it was impossible to keep them safe.

> *As the Quran says "Indeed Pharaoh arrogantly elevated himself in the land and divided its people into subservient groups, one of which he persecuted, slaughtering their sons and keeping their women. He was truly one of the corruptors." (Quran 28:4)*

However, the All-Powerful Allah (SWT) al-Muqtadir decided to support the same individuals who Pharaoh was persecuting:

> *"But it was Our Will to favor those who were oppressed in the land, making them models of faith as well as successors; and to establish them in the land; and through them show Pharaoh, Hamân, and their soldiers the fulfillment of what they feared." (Quran 28:5-6)*

Thus, the real mother of Musa (AS) was in a panic when Musa (AS) was born in the designated year. However, Allah (SWT) sent Hazrat Jibrail (AS) to console her, tell her to have faith in Allah (SWT), and set the infant adrift on the Nile in a basket.

> *We inspired the mother of Moses: "Nurse him, but when you fear for him, put him then into the river, and do not fear or grieve. We will certainly return him to you, and make him one of the messengers." (Quran 28:7)*

She followed directions but was distraught. Her heart was fortified by Allah (SWT), yet she almost made the matter public. She urged her daughter Miriam to keep an eye out for any updates regarding the baby and kept her loss a secret from the rest of the family. Miriam quickly located the baby.

> *And the heart of Moses' mother ached so much that she almost gave away his identity, had We not reassured her heart in order for her to have faith in Allah's promise. And she said to his sister, "Keep track of him!" So she watched him from a distance, while they were unaware.*
> *(Quran 28:10-11)*

This marked the beginning of Hazrat Asiya's (RA) role. Despite Pharaoh's reluctance, she was able to persuade Pharaoh not to kill the child. The timing could not have been more ideal: Musa was rejecting milk from every woman brought to Asiya's house. Thankfully, wet-nursing—the practice of nursing babies by women other than their biological mothers—was widespread back then. Miriam then offered her mother's house and wet-nursing services after spotting Asiya's staff at the neighbourhood market:

> *And We had caused him to refuse all wet-nurses at first, so his sister suggested, "Shall I direct you to a family who will bring him up for you and take good care of him?"*
> *(Quran 28:12)*

The servants first doubted Mariam's motives, but she persuaded them that she and her family solely had Pharaoh's best interests in mind, according to Ibn Kathir. As Allah (SWT) had promised, Musa returned to his birth mother's house for a while, and she fed him.

> *"This is how we returned him to his mother so that her heart would be put at ease, and not grieve, and that she would know that Allah's promise is always true. But most people do not know". (Quran 28:13)*

This is how Musa (AS) was raised in the Pharaoh's court under the watchful eye of Hazrat Asiya (RA), with his sister serving as his playmate and his mother as his wet nurse. The Pharaoh, frequently wary of the infant, kept a close watch on Musa (AS). But with Allah's (SWT) assistance, Hazrat Asiya (RA) was able to keep him safe.

Legacy and Veneration: Asiya as a Role Model

The Pharaoh was enraged when Musa (AS) challenged his beliefs, but Asiya (RA) embraced Islam without hesitation and said nothing. For years, she spent years living in Pharaoh's home as a covert Muslim. She maintained her secrecy without any issues until one evening when she defended her convictions.

Earlier that day, Pharaoh's daughter (not through Asiya RA) was in the palace having her hair combed by her maid when the maid dropped the hairbrush due to clumsiness. As the brush dropped to the ground, the maid said, "May Allah's curse be on those who claim to be gods. The Pharaoh's daughter turned to her immediately and asked, "Do you believe in a god besides my father?"

"The One Allah, who has no partners, is my Allah, your Allah, your father's Allah, and the Allah of the heavens and the earth," the maid declared. Pharaoh's daughter, known for her gossip, immediately went to her father and reported exactly what the maid had said.

To make an example of her, Pharaoh ordered the maid's entire family to be burned in front of the entire city. As the flames consumed them, the moment came for the newborn to face the same fate, Allah (SWT) performed a miracle—her child spoke, stating that the torment in this world is less than the torment in the next. The poor mother witnessed her children being burned in front of her very eyes.

This heartbreaking scene ignited the flame of Islam in Asiya's (RA) heart. Witnessing the maid-servant's unwavering faith, she embraced

Islam. That very evening, she went to Pharaoh and declared her faith, rejecting him and his false claims.

Even his own wife embraced Islam and believed in Allah! He could not stand it. Unable to tolerate her defiance, Asiya (RA) was shackled to the ground and dragged to the desert by Pharaoh. There, the daughters of Pharaoh's concubines would visit her every day to mock and laugh at her, and she was denied food, water, and shade.

Asiya (RA) gazed up at the sky and murmured, "Oh Allah, build for me with you a palace in Jannah."

Allah (SWT) then gave Angel Jibreel the order to show Asiya (RA) her palace in Jannah. She was filled with happiness and tranquillity at witnessing this and quietly departed from this life.

Unaware that she was already dead, Pharaoh gave the order to crush her to death by dropping a massive boulder on her. They took this action, but her soul had already left and was basking in Paradise's benefits.

We may learn a lot from Asiya (RA), one of the four outstanding women of Jannah. Even though she was extremely wealthy and powerful, this aristocratic woman quickly converted to Islam after realising the truth.

Both men and women can learn timeless lessons from Asiya's (RA) life. She is a living example of the strength of faith and bravery, demonstrating that loyalty to Allah, rather than financial prosperity or social standing, is the ultimate measure of success. Her perseverance in the face of extreme hardship encourages believers to put their faith above material worries.

Asiya's (RA) legacy reminds us that in a world full of injustice, the greatest victory is to hold firmly to our convictions and pursue Allah's pleasure. Her unwavering devotion makes her a timeless role model for humanity and continues to inspire many believers.

Chapter Three

The Legacy of Razia Sultana

Long ago, in 1205, a courageous queen named Razia Sultana reigned. As the first female monarch of the Delhi Sultanate, she was unique, independent, friendly, and incredibly intelligent. When she was in power, she improved the nation's arts, education, and governance, which benefited her people. Razia Sultana overcame many obstacles, but her bravery and tenacity inspired others.

She was the first Muslim woman ruler in India, serving as the Sultan of Delhi from 1236 to 1240. This title and position of authority had never been granted to a woman. As the sixth Mamluk Sultan, she was one of the rare female rulers in the history of Islamic civilisations worldwide.

The Delhi Sultanate: A Brief Overview

The Delhi Sultanate was a Muslim empire that ruled north India. Because it was ruled by a sultan, the state is known as a sultanate. The Delhi Sultanate was established after the victory over the Rajput monarchs. These monarchs eventually constructed several cities in the Delhi region as their capital. Notwithstanding obstacles like internal conflict and Mongol invasions, the Delhi Sultanate was instrumental in forming India's history.

Delhi rose to prominence in India in the twelfth century. In the middle of the 12th century, the Chauhans of Ajmer overran the capital city of the Tomara Rajputs. The Delhi Sultanate was established in 1192 when Mohamed Ghori overthrew Prithviraj Chauhan and took Delhi.

Before 1000 AD, the Hindu and Buddhist kingdoms dominated India. However, invasions from Central Asia, notably Afghanistan, began in 962 AD. These invasions and attacks persisted for many years without establishing the kingdom's permanent borders.

In 1173, Muhammad Ghori established his kingdom after launching a concerted assault to extend his dominion over northern India. Following Ghori's death in 1206, Qutb-ud-din Aibak, a Turkic Mamluk, became Delhi's first sultan.

With his family of rulers, known as the Slave Dynasty, he helped establish the Delhi Sultanate. The region was later governed by numerous other prominent Delhi sultanate dynasties. Aibak ruled as sultan from 1206 to 1210 and was succeeded by Aram Shah, who held the position for just a year. Over the following three centuries, the Delhi Sultanate expanded until 1526 when Ibrahim Lodi lost the combat of Panipat to Babur, bringing an end to the Delhi Sultanate.

Qutb-ud-din Aibak, who himself had ascended from slavery to positions of authority, placed a premium on intellect, intelligence, and organisational skills in people. Due to his abundance of these attributes, Iltutmish was able to marry Aibak's daughter and become the governor of the Badaun area.

The Turkic nobles of Lahore quickly installed his son Aram on the throne after Aibak unexpectedly passed away in 1210 while playing chovgan, a type of horseback polo. The Delhi officials were unhappy with this choice and offered the throne to the late sultan's son-in-law, Iltutmish. In 1211, the Iltutmish invaded Delhi, routed Aram-Shah's army, took him prisoner, and took the crown.

The Iltutmish grew and fortified the sultanate, establishing Delhi as its capital and the Delhi Sultanate as an independent kingdom. He severed the dynasty's political ties with the Ghur and constructed waterworks, mosques, and other facilities to make Delhi a suitable seat of administration for the first time. He also finished building the Qutb Minar, Delhi's famous victory tower, which Aibak had started. The Qutb Minar is one of Asia's tallest minarets—towers from which Muslims are summoned to prayer.

During his rule, Iltutmish faced three issues. First, he had to protect the western boundary. Second, he had to subdue the Muslim aristocrats in India. Third, he had to conquer several Hindu lords who continued to have some autonomy. In all three categories, Iltutmish had a fair amount of success.

The ruler's family life was also going well. After his principal wife, Turkan Khatun, the daughter of Aibak, gave birth to his daughter Razia, he had four boys from his other spouses. Iltutmish's children received an equal education, learning the sciences, archery, riding horses, military tactics, and government.

However, Nasir-ud-din Mahmud, his oldest son and governor of Bengal, was regarded as his main ally and heir apparent. Mahmud died in 1229, long before his father, so he was not meant to become the Sultan of Delhi. Iltutmish chose to bequeath the throne to his daughter Razia because the other children did not inspire much optimism.

However, the Turkish Muslim aristocrats who had served as Iltutmish's advisors and slaves protested against having a woman in charge. The nobility questioned this choice, claiming that the ruler still had sons. According to historian Minhaj-i-Siraj, Iltutmish retorted that he valued Razia's skills more than his sons'. We can only surmise whether this mythology is real or was made up by Razia's adherents during the throne race.

When the sultan placed Razia in charge of the Delhi government for his battle against Gwalior in 1231, she had already demonstrated her capacity for sensible governance. Iltutmish gave his commander, Mushrif-i Mamlakat Taj al-Mulk Mahmud Dabir, instructions to draft a decree designating Razia as his heir after observing how skilfully she carried out her tasks. When he died in 1236, she ascended to the crown. The populace backed Razia.

Shah Turkan was taken into custody by an angry mob that overran the royal palace. The state's major army and a number of aristocrats pledged loyalty to Razia. After a rule that lasted less than seven months, Rukn-ud-din went to Delhi but was soon captured, imprisoned, and put to death—either by soldiers or by Delhi inhabitants who attacked the mosque where he was hiding. As a result, in November 1236, Razia, or more specifically Jalalat-ud-din Razia Sultan bint Iltutmish, emerged as the first Muslim monarch in South Asia.

Razia's Rise to Power: Breaking Gender Norms

The great ruler Sultan Razia possessed all the noble qualities and qualifications required of a king, including wisdom, fairness, beneficence, patronage of the learnt, administration of justice, love for her citizens, and warlike ability. She possessed every attribute a monarch should have, but because she was not of the appropriate sex, men saw no value in these attributes.

For the first time in Indian history, a monarch selected a woman to take his place as heir. Even more important is the fact that it was his "choice" and not the result of "political pressure." As Iltutmish is quoted by Minhaj-i-Siraj, "My sons devote themselves to the pleasures of youthfulness, and not one of them meets the requirements to be king. You will discover that my daughter is the most qualified individual to lead the State after my passing, and they are unqualified to govern the nation."

From her childhood, Iltutmish ensured Razia received instruction in the arts of administration, diplomacy, horsemanship, and warfare on par with his sons. His reliable and skilled Abyssinian slaver, Malik

Yaqut, oversaw her training. However, Razia never truly adopted the traditional behaviour expected of modern Muslim women because she spent little time in the harem (with the ladies of the household).

She desired to be regarded as a true Sultan, a ruler and leader in her own right. Much to the chagrin of the orthodox forces at court, she is believed to have removed the veil (purdah) and chose to show her face in public. Rejecting feminine attire, she instead donned men's robes, a tunic, and a turban—garments befitting a Sultan.

She helped her father on several occasions and actively participated in state matters. Since women were not regarded as worthy of positions of power in those days, Razia consciously distanced herself from being just a woman once she attained a position of responsibility and respect. Raziya Sultan's father encouraged her to become interested in the army's structure and assumed charge, which helped her develop her leadership, responsibility, and courageous skills.

Challenges and Rebellion: The Struggles of a Female Ruler

Even though her reign (1236–1240) was short, it was full of difficulties and uprisings, underscoring the tremendous difficulties a woman in medieval India faced when trying to lead a large and intricate empire.

Naturally, she made a lot of enemies because of her success and gender. The promotion of an Abyssinian slave named Jamal-ud-Din Yaqut to a high post on her court was one of her most contentious choices. The Turkish nobility, who saw this action as an insult to their privileged position, were incensed. Razia's opponents likely made up rumours of a romantic connection between her and Yaqut to challenge her legitimacy as a queen and weaken her authority.

It was sufficient for the kadis (judges) to declare that Razia Sultan had broken Shariah law and ought to resign as ruler when it started to be rumoured that she had fallen in love with Jamaluddin Yaqut, an African slave of the court.

Due to these difficulties, a revolt developed. Delhi was surrounded by rebels, and Razia's army was not enough. The capital appeared poised to fall, and the first Muslim sultan's authority was about to crumble. However, Razia was adept at both diplomacy and the art of battle. After leading her soldiers from the city, she made camp on the Yamuna River's banks. Her primary objective was to negotiate secretly rather than combat with the opponent.

The governor of the citadel of Sadusan and the ruler of Lahore eventually sided with her. While the other rebel commanders escaped, several of them were quickly apprehended and put to death. As Razia's position grew stronger, the aristocracy who backed her believed she would become a nominal monarch.

Even while the people of Delhi genuinely loved their gifted and righteous queen, Razia had many opponents because traditional Muslims saw her actions as immoral and too permissive and her attempts to challenge the patriarchal system's established norms outraged them. The Shia community, which at the time was far more extreme than the Sunnis in India, opposed Razia in particular.

Razia also encountered prejudice in society stemming from gender stereotypes. Although her daring display of power was criticised, her decision to forgo customary feminine dress in favour of masculine royal clothing was also criticised. Conservative forces in her court and society at large opposed her attempts to defy gender norms and rule as a sovereign ruler rather than a figurehead.

In 1237, Razia faced political unrest. On March 5, Shias stormed Delhi's largest mosque, and about a thousand people from Delhi, Sindh, Gujarat, and Doab joined their leader, Nuruddin Turk. In retaliation, the locals, mostly Sunnis who had assembled for Friday prayers, slaughtered the Shia rebels.

Izz-ud-din was compelled to submit and once more recognise Razia's power after Razia's army triumphed. When Razia came to Delhi on April 3, 1240, she discovered that the Turkic nobility had incited a revolt against her by Ikhtiyar-ud-din Altunia, the ruler of Bhatinda (the Punjab region), a former slave whom she had exalted. She launched a campaign opposing him, but it was unsuccessful. Razia's reign came to a tragic end in 1240 when she was slain, outnumbered and deserted by her allies.

Razia's Legacy: The First and Only Female Sultan of Delhi

Razia was a strong and confident leader, exactly as Iltutmish had envisioned. She was a brave warrior who led troops from the front in battles and conquered new lands, enhancing her nation's reputation and strength. Legend has it that she bravely rode an elephant into battle while leading her army. Minting money was a sign of control and sovereignty in the Muslim world at the time, so she made the easy decision to show off her power by issuing coins in her name, just like any other strong leader.

By laying the foundation for several public libraries and educational facilities, Razia also improved the general well-being of the populace. Her strategy was secular throughout because the education system in these institutions was designed to impart knowledge of traditional scientific and literary works from various civilisations.

Razia, Delhi's first female monarch, continues to be incredibly well-known in popular culture. She has been the focus of numerous Bollywood films and TV shows, and numerous books have been written about her life and times. However, only a small number of these pieces truly provide a comprehensive picture of the courageous and aspirational woman she was. It would be a great injustice to diminish the memory of such a magnificent woman since she never meekly accepted the conventions but instead questioned them at every turn.

Despite living in a firmly patriarchal environment, this woman made a name for herself, followed her heart without regard for what others might think, ruled without the help of a father, husband, or son, and worked to better not only her own situation but also that of all the women in her domain by leading by example.

Razia Sultan is and will continue to be an inspiration to the next generation of both men and women, both as a woman and a ruler. After all, Razia is the only person Minhaj-i-Siraj recognised as a Lashgarkash, or military leader, in the lengthy list of Iltutmish dynasty monarchs.

Chapter Four

Sultanah Taj ul-Alam Safiatuddin Syah of Aceh

An important character in Aceh and Southeast Asian history was Sultanah Taj ul-Alam Safiatuddin Syah (1641–1675). Following the passing of her spouse, Sultan Iskandar Thani, she became the first woman to hold the throne of the Aceh Sultanate. A crucial juncture in Aceh's history, her rule was distinguished by stability in politics, economic growth, and Aceh's strategic significance in regional and international geopolitics.

In a time when female leadership was rare in the Muslim world, Sultanah Safiatuddin's reign was revolutionary. Her ascension proved Aceh's cultural adaptability and the social impact of matrilineal customs. She maintained the sultanate's central authority and promoted political unity by deftly navigating internal conflicts.

Despite early opposition, Aceh's influential ulema (Islamic academics) and nobility supported her because of her ability as a ruler. Under her direction, Aceh remained a hub of Islamic scholarship and culture, drawing traders and academics from all over the Muslim world. Safiatuddin balanced the interests of many factions within her realm by promoting religious research and upholding Islamic ideals while taking a practical approach to governing.

Sultanah Taj ul-Alam Safiatuddin was the first of four queens to rule the kingdom of Aceh in succession. She would set the bar high for all who followed her. She was the longest ruling monarch in Aceh at the time, successfully ruling her kingdom for 35 years. She was not only a figurehead but a successful ruler in her own right, navigating a turbulent sea and satisfying the elite and European colonists while guaranteeing her nation's wealth and prosperity.

Aceh's Strategic Importance in Southeast Asia

Aceh is located in the northernmost portion of Sumatra, now a province of the Republic of Indonesia. While it is known to Europeans as Acheen, Aceh is the proper name for the region of Sumatra that stretches from Tamiang Point on the east coast to Trumon on the west coast. However, this geographical concept was only applicable after the fifteenth century. In its early history, Aceh referred to what is known as "Aceh Proper," the northwest district encompassing the Atjeh River and its port of Atjeh.

In Dàr al-Kamàl, the hinterland at the northernmost point of the region, which is roughly a mile from the coast, Aceh may have once been the name of a tiny kingdom. Since Aceh was an inland kingdom, few foreign traders or tourists were aware of it or had ever been there.

Although we are unaware who founded it, the kingdom itself had to have emerged by the end of the 14th century. Following its merger with Lamuri of Mahkota Àlam around the close of the fifteenth or early sixteenth centuries, early indications of Aceh's rise can be seen. In general, two features were noteworthy in relation to the formation of the Aceh Sultanate's new power structure. These were the region's economic potential and geostrategic location.

Aceh's strategic importance in Southeast Asia just before the ruler Sulṭāna Taj ul-Alam Safiatuddin Syah was recorded unparalleled in history. Aceh became a prominent region and gained supremacy in international partnerships in international trade, primarily due to its state structure and geostrategic location on the far northwest of Sumatra.

This allowed Aceh to participate in the international sea trade among the east and the west in the 16th and 19th centuries. Situated at the northern tip of Sumatra, it commanded the Strait of Malacca, one of the world's busiest trade routes.

As a hub for Islamic learning and culture, Aceh was dubbed the "Veranda of Mecca," and its cultural and theological prominence contributed to its economic wealth. Leaders like Sultan Iskandar Muda, who increased Aceh's territory and fortified its naval superiority, saw the peak of Aceh's political supremacy.

The powerful navy of the kingdom became famous for its active role in protecting trade routes and defending against Portuguese and other colonial invasions. Aceh became a pillar of Southeast Asia's geopolitical landscape and established the groundwork for its lasting legacy with its combination of economic prosperity, military prowess, and religious prominence.

The Reign of Sultanah Taj ul-Alam: A New Era

Taj ul-Alam Safiatuddin Syah was born in 1612 to Iskandar Muda, the king of Aceh (modern-day Indonesia), and his royal bride Putri Sani. Although her father's reign was referred to as Aceh's "golden age," he was a despot who used force rather than diplomacy to rule. Tragically, he had killed his own son just months before his own death, leaving no eligible male heirs. He therefore nominated his son-in-law, Iskandar Thani, to ascend to the throne after his passing.

Iskandar Thani was a flamboyant and extravagant ruler whose reign led to the depletion of the royal coffers due to his lavish ordering of expensive jewellery from the Dutch. The youthful sultan passed away suddenly after only five years in rule, most likely as a consequence of an assassination. His foreign origin, extravagant lifestyle, and the harshness of his reign—during which he had planned the murders of up to 400 possible opponents—made him an unpopular monarch. Thani's passing created a power vacuum and an ambiguous succession plan.

Since there were no male successors who were genuine and had a proper royal history, his death caused a crisis. Amidst the turmoil, various figures, including Orang Kaya, declared themselves king, unwilling to see one of their own ascend the throne. However, it was Safiatuddin, the widow of Iskandar Thani and the daughter of Iskander Muda, who became the focus of attention.

Three days after her husband's passing, she ascended to the throne in the wake of discussions concerning whether a female ruler could be allowed under Islamic law. Sultanah Taj ul-Alam Safiatuddin Syah, which translates to "world crown, purity of the faith," replaced her given name, Putri Sri Alam.

The Dutch East India Company was gradually gaining control of nearby lands, therefore she inherited a troubled monarchy. Aceh resisted the strain and even kept their vassal states in spite of multiple political conflicts with the Dutch, who were attempting to obtain a monopoly on the trade in tin and pepper.

One of the most significant was with Perak, a rich tin-producing state in Malaysia, where Aceh held economic and strategic interest.

Aceh was a significant pepper trading hub and the most important Muslim economic hub in the entire Mediterranean region.

By utilising connections with other Muslim nations and cultivating economic ties with a variety of partners, such as the Ottoman Turks,

Persia, and India, Safiatuddin's administration was able to preserve Aceh's independence. Under her rule, Aceh stood as a symbol of defiance against European colonialism, showcasing both the resilience of its people and the strategic thinking of its rulers.

Diplomacy and Resilience: Her Strategic Leadership

The Dutch East India Company (VOC) requested reimbursement for an expensive jewellery set that her late husband, the former Sultan, had commissioned. Safiatuddin, who had a more sensible perspective on Aceh's financial situation, declined to take the necklace, claiming it was useless for women because it was made for men.

Nevertheless, VOC representatives pushed for payment. Safiatuddin eventually negotiated a compromise that ended hostilities and permitted the VOC to decrease their losses after drawing out the situation for four years and interacting with multiple envoys dispatched from Holland. But she did not let them preserve face completely.

Later in her tenure, another issue broke out. By blocking the Perak River, the VOC was attempting to monopolise Perak's tin resources with increasing vigour. On May 6, 1651, a yacht that was blockading the river reported that the VOC warehouse had been robbed and the crew members of two Dutch ships had been killed.

Suspecting Acehnese collusion, the Dutch commissioner put pressure on Safiatuddin to look into the issue and demanded guarantees of safety, restitution for their losses, and accountability for their deceased. Safiatuddin was thus forced to choose between defending Aceh, standing by Perak, and preserving amicable ties with the VOC.

In 1655, a year after the passing of her allies, including the Sultan of Perak, the matter was ultimately resolved in a contract.

Because of her skillful diplomacy in resolving disputes and defending Acehnese identity during a time of violent and widespread European colonisation, her 34-year reign was renowned for its stability and tranquillity. During that time, it was common for an authority to end when the king or queen was deposed or killed. Furthermore, Safiatuddin's reign is recognised as the start of an era of excellence of Islamic scholarship in the areas of the arts and education.

The Influence of Female Leadership in Aceh

Aceh's economy thrived under the sage guidance of Sultanah Taj ul-Alam. The area developed into a significant trading hub that drew traders from both sides of the Indian Ocean. The Sultanah maintained close relations with nearby Islamic kingdoms and promoted trade with European countries, such as the Dutch and the British. Roads, bridges, and canals were among the several infrastructure projects in which Sultanah Taj ul-Alam made significant investments. These developments made the region's commerce, communication, and trade easier.

There were two opposing schools of Islamic thinking in Aceh during the time, each shaping the spiritual and political landscape of the region. The first faction adhered to Wahdatul Wujud, a mystical concept of unity of existence that was widely accepted and championed by Hamzah Fansuri and his followers.

This school of thought enjoyed significant support from Sultan Iskandar Muda, who was known for his patronage of intellectual and cultural pursuits. The second faction, led by Sheikh Nuruddin Al Raniri, adhered to a more orthodox and puritanical interpretation of Islam. Despite its stricter approach, this party found greater favor with Sultan Iskandar Thani, who was inclined toward a more conservative religious framework.

Sultanah Safiatuddin allowed religious clerics to handle their own religious matters and showed no preference for any one group. She did not take sides because she understood religion should not be politicised. The advancement of Islam in Aceh is one of her most notable contributions. She sent scholars to India, Baghdad, Medina, and Makkah to study Islam. She exhorted religious scholars to create books with diligence. She actually wrote a book called "Masail Al Muktadi." To propagate Islam, she dispatched missionaries from Aceh to Siam.

To protect the kingdom of Aceh, the Sultanah has also organised a special army of women. She also appointed women to the Court of Justice, another aspect of the judiciary. Future queens were made possible by the successful 35-year reign of Sultana Taj ul-Alam Safiatuddin Syah in Aceh. According to Dutch academics, Aceh felt like a female monarch had always controlled the country during the Queen's reign. She was succeeded by three queens after her death in 1675.

Chapter Five

Nur Jahan: The Power behind the Mughal Throne

Some historians consider Nur Jahan, or Mehr-un-Nissa, the chief spouse of Mughal emperor Jahangir to have been the real force behind the throne for a large portion of her husband's rule. Nur Jahan was the most well-liked Mughal Empress.

The Mughal Empire reached its zenith thanks to her contributions to literature, art, and the social and cultural mores of the day. On her own merit, she ascended from lowly origins to become the de facto head of the Mughal Empire. She may have been the initial and sole Mughal empress to have a position of authority over the king. Historians are interested in her colourful life and works.

The Mughal Empire: Context and Expansion

The Eurasian landmass includes the South Asian subcontinent, which provides for present-day Bangladesh, Pakistan, Afghanistan, and Sri Lanka. It has a lengthy history of little states and large empires, much like Europe. It was mostly run by a loose union of wealthy port cities and strong princely states in 1750. There was a period when the powerful Mughal Empire ruled the subcontinent.

The Mughal Empire was founded by Prince Babur. Babur was born in Central Asia as a royal. He took control of the region known as Ferghana, a city in present-day Uzbekistan, at the age of just twelve. This indicated that he developed into a proficient and successful fighter at a very young age. Babur established the Mughal Empire in 1526 after leading his army southward and seizing Delhi. Babur engaged in numerous conflicts to seize control of India's northern region over the course of the following four years. Even though he prevailed in these conflicts, it cost him dearly. Babur passed away from natural causes after just four years, leaving the Mughal Empire with inadequate money.

Babur's son, Humayun, succeeded his father as emperor. At the time, the Mughal Empire was only developing, and it required a capable military leader to safeguard and prosper. Following his 1544 alliance with Emperor Ṭahmāsp in Iran, Humayun returned to India with his newly formed army and seized Delhi and Lahore in 1555.

However, because he favoured poetry over fighting or commanding his army in battle, Humayun was viewed as a weak military figurehead. He was exiled from 1540 to 1555 and endured numerous challenges from his half-brothers. Sadly, the following year, he passed away in an accident after tumbling down the stairs in front of his library.

Akbar seized power in the Mughal Empire in 1556. By the conclusion of his rule, Akbar had extended the empire to encompass the majority of present-day India, although at this time it only included the Punjab and a tiny region surrounding Delhi. Many historians regard his reign as the Mughal Empire's "Golden Age." Since he was only 13, his guardian oversaw the empire for the first five years. However, after compelling his protector, Bairam Khan, to retire, Akbar rapidly established himself as a powerful monarch when he was just eighteen.

Following Akbar's reign, his son Jahangir continued his father's policy of religious tolerance toward Hinduism and his administrative structure. Under his support, Mughal painting achieved a high degree of beauty and grandeur, and he constructed magnificent gardens and monuments. The British built the first industries in India in 1611, signalling the start of European influence.

In 1611, Jahangir wed Nur Jahan, also known as the "Light of the World." Shah Jahan, his son, ascended to the throne shortly after his demise in October 1627. He inherited a huge and prosperous empire that was arguably the biggest in history at the middle of the century and displayed a level of centralised authority that had rarely been seen before.

Following his son Aurangzeb's victory, the Mughal Empire began to fall apart in the latter half of the seventeenth century, but it experienced additional growth in the early years of his lengthy rule (1658–1707). Many of Aurangzeb's vassals became independent kings after his death in 1707, marking the start of the era known as "successor states."

Although the Mughal Empire lasted until 1857, its monarchs were East India Company pensioners after 1803. The elderly Bahadur Shah Zafar, the final emperor, was tried for allegedly inciting sedition and leading the rebels in the 1857 revolt. After being found guilty, he was sent to Rangoon to live the rest of his days in a foreign land.

The Mughals were a Muslim dynasty that ruled over a predominantly Hindu populace. By 1750, they had ruled over a large portion of South Asia for many years. When the Mughals first came to India, Muslims were already there. Although Muslims made up only 15% of the population during the Mughal era, the Mughals accepted all local religions for the majority of their time in power. The program established enough social stability to guarantee prosperous trade, investment, and business.

However, the Mughals' authority started to shift in the middle of the seventeenth century for two reasons. First, the central government of the waning empire was challenged by various groups due to widening internal conflicts. Second, governments and traders in Europe began searching for methods to share in the empire's wealth.

Mehr-un-Nissa to Nur Jahan: The Journey to Empress

The 18th and final wife of the fourth Mughal monarch Jahangir, Nur Jahan (formerly Mehr-un-Nissa) served as the Empress consort of the Mughal kingdom from 25 May 1611 until 28 October 1627.

Nur Jahan was born to Mirza Giyaz Beg and Asmat Begam. Out of the four children, she was the second daughter. In Afghanistan, Mirza Giyaz Beg had a business. Regretfully, he suffered a significant commercial loss, which led the family to go to India. During their journey, they were ambushed by thieves halfway through their journey. There was no food left for the household. Mehr-un-Nissa was born amidst these hardship after the family arrived in Kandahar.

The family's fortunes changed when they were assisted by Malik Masud, a wealthy merchant who was leading a caravan. He arranged a job for Mehr-un-Nissa's father in the Mughan court of Emperor Akbar, which altered their fate. It was at the time Mehr-un-Nissa was named "Sun among Women", acknowledging that the child's birth marked a turning point in their destiny.

She received the best education possible from her parents, learning Arabic and Persian, and developing a strong interest in administration. She was also skilled in dancing, art, and literature.

At the age of 17, she married Ali Quli Istajlu, who was killed ten years later. Following his death in 1607, she and her daughter Ladli Begum were called to the court of Emperor Akbar's son Jahangir to serve as the Dowager Empress.

In 1611, during the springtime festival of Navroz, which marked the start of the New Year, Nur Jahan reconnected with Emperor Jahangir at the royal residence meena bazaar. After a brief courtship, they married on May 25 of the same year Jahangir proposed had right away. At the beginning of her second marriage, she was thirty-four years old and would become Jahangir's eighteenth and final lawful wife. The titles Nur Mahal (Light of the Palace) and Nur Jahan (Light of the Globe) were bestowed upon her after her marriage.

Nur Jahan's Influence: Administration and Politics

In addition to ruling over the heart, Nur Jahan ruled alongside Jahangir, holding significant sway over the empire.

Jahangir's reign was marked by contradictions; his heart was as contradictory as the kaleidoscopic nation he controlled. As much as Jahangir's poor health and weakness are due to his alcoholism, he also owes his many years of calm rule to Nur Jahan. She became his preferred companion and wife, greatly aiding him in managing the state's affairs.

Emperor Jehangir did, in fact, have such faith in her wisdom and judgement that he progressively let his Queen govern the nation and gave himself up increasingly to his own "pleasures." Thus, Nur Jahan would lead the Council of State, give directives, and make choices that had an impact on the entire nation. Her great administrative skills and strong sense of duty won her admiration and respect.

To strengthen her status and authority, she persuaded her husband to appoint her several family members to important positions in the court and administrative departments. She appointed her brother Asaf Khan as Jahangir's great Wazir, or minister. She also arranged for her daughter Ladli to wed Jahangir's youngest son Shahryar. The expansion of Nur Jahan's family's power within the Mughal Empire was guaranteed by this marriage.

Gaining a significant advantage over her husband, she assumed joint leadership of the kingdom and used her political power with shrewdness, bravery, and wisdom. In a comparatively short time, she rose to prominence at the court and quickly rose to become a strong, resourceful, and respected woman.

During Nur Jahan's rule, trade expanded and Agra became a significant commercial centre. Nur Jahan established profitable trading connections in Asia and Europe and commanded the collection of levies on products from traders and merchants. Throughout the Mughal kingdom, she ordered the building of numerous sarais, or rest areas, for traders. She also amassed an enormous fortune outside of the Mughal treasury by owning ships in her name that she used to ferry pilgrims to Mecca and goods to Europe.

Cultural Patronage: Nur Jahan's Legacy in Art and Architecture

She had proven to be equally competent in commercial and trade-related issues in addition to her administrative abilities. Among her many talents were her love of textiles, singing, and architectural design. Nur Jahan added fresh subjects to the Mughal fabric and preferred representational painting, which may have reflected the more iconic art in her native Persia. Several new paintings with subjects not previously depicted in Mughal India were produced by her fusing her creative vision with inspiration from the secular subjects arriving from Europe. She questioned and pushed the social and cultural norms of her time to their boundaries without violating them.

Nur Jahan was a distinguished woman with a wide range of interests. She was particularly skilled at singing and playing musical instruments. Because of her achievements, she was a popular companion, and her taste went beyond supporting artists and architects. She designed and created new patterns for palace interiors, room decorations, gold decorations, brocades, carpets, lace, gowns, and dresses, ensuring that the women's fashions of her era were still popular.

Nur Jahan became a role model for the ladies of royalty and enjoyed planning elaborate feasts. She also took care of the underprivileged and destitute and championed the cause of orphan girls. She was supposedly a social worker who generously helped many poor applicants, particularly those without dowries. Her influence brought much renowned Persian nobility to the Mughal court.

Nur Jahan also established numerous private and public gardens across the empire. Regretfully, some of these might have been lost over time. It is not easy to maintain a garden that is healthy and nurtured for five hundred years. All that is left are descriptions of their potential appearance and the animals they might have housed.

Chapter Six

Shajar al-Durr: The Queen of Egypt

The first and only woman to hold the Islamic Egyptian throne was Shajara al-Durr (r. 1250), who founded the Mamluk Dynasty in Egypt. Although she was only sultan for eighty days, she made a lasting impression with architectural monuments featuring her emblem, a tree with gold inlay and mother-of-pearl linings.

This woman became Egypt's first female Muslim monarch and the first woman to be named a Sultan after rising from the slave ranks. Shajar as-Durr is known as the "Tree of Pearls".

The Ayyubid Dynasty and the Mamluk Rise

The Kurdish Zangid warrior Salah al-Din (r. 1169–93), or Saladin as he is known in Europe, led the Ayyubid dynasty to power. He proclaimed the end of the Fatimid caliphate and created the Ayyubid Sultanate (1171) after driving out a Crusader army that had advanced to the gates of Fatimid Cairo and was seizing Egypt on behalf of the Zangids (1160s). Soon after, Salah al-Din also took over Syria in the 1180s and Yemen in 1174.

The Turkic mamluks were largely responsible for the end of the dynasty, as they deposed Turan Shah (r. 1249–50), the last self-directed Ayyubid sultan in Egypt, and established the Mamluk Sultanate (1250–1517). The sultanate relied on mamluks, or slave troops, to organise its military.

In 1250, a group of slave warriors, the Mamluks, took control of Egypt. The fertile Levantine and Egyptian regions were under the Mamluk Sultanate's dominion. It also contained the holy cities of Mecca, Medina, and Jerusalem in Islam. Because of these assets, the sultanate was one of the most powerful and important governments of its era.

The Mamluk Sultanate developed into the dominant Islamic state of its era. The Mamluks gained prominence in the 13th century and established dominance by fending off Mongol and Crusader invasions. The sultanate expanded into a kingdom with millions of subjects throughout the centuries.

The Arabic word Mamluk means "one who is owned", slaves of non-Arab descent. The Mamluks were bought when they were still young boys and began their life as slaves. Because of their intense dependence on their lords, Mamluks were regarded as obedient subjects. Young Mamluks living far from home lacked political and social ties that would have weakened their allegiance. This made it safe for slave owners, such as the sultan and strong emirs, to shape their Mamluks into intelligent and competent individuals by teaching those Islamic sciences, martial arts, and court etiquette, among other things.

Mamluks were released after finishing their schooling but were still expected to stay faithful to their family and patron. They could rise to positions of prominence now that they were part of the sultanate's military elite. Even several of the Mamluk Empire's sultans were once slaves. Prior to the rise of the Mamluk Sultanate in Egypt, the Islamic world had been buying and training Mamluks for generations, but they had never before taken control of a sizable portion of the political landscape. The Ayyubid Sultan As-Salih Ayyub was the focal point of their 1250 sultanate claim in Cairo.

As-Salih decided to purchase a significant amount of Turkic as well as Caucasian Mamluks because he had a tenuous hold on power and was involved in political intrigues. He could solidify his power now that he had a powerful military. As-Salih fought against other Ayyubid kingdoms and crusaders from 1240 to 1249. Throughout this period, he made excellent use of his Mamluks, who were the core of his army.

Al-Muazzam Turanshah, As-Salih's son, succeeded him shortly after his death in November 1249. The new sultan probably had no idea how powerful the Mamluks had grown in the preceding years. Turanshah elevated the Kurdish warriors he brought to positions of authority after he arrived in Egypt. Turanshash was assassinated by a group of conspirators in retaliation, with Baibars, a well-known Mamluk chieftain, delivering the final blow. Aybak, a Mamluk commander, wed As-Salih's widow after Turanshah's death. The Mamluk Sultanate was formally created in 1250 when she ceded the throne to Aybak.

Shajar al-Durr's Ascension: From Slave to Sultana

Although Shajara al-Durr's exact birthdate is unknown due to a dearth of evidence, some historians assume that she was born in what is now Armenia, perhaps just before 1230 CE. She was enslaved and originally came from the Qipchaq (Kipchak) tribe of the steppes of modern-day southern Russia.

When she was eleven years old, she was taken from Baghdad to either Damascus or Cairo, whereupon she was given as a present to the young governor of Hisn Kayfa, al-Salih Ayyub (r. 1240 & 1245-9). Concubines were regarded as suitable presents for allies. But after meeting the prince, Shajara al-Durr's life took a different turn.

The young slave girl joined al-Salih in the royal harem, as was customary at the time. She soon became his favourite friend, and the future sultan adored her so much that he would never go anywhere without her. Before Shajar al-Durr entered As-Salih Ayoubbi's harem, she was considered attractive, intellectual, and well-educated. In a

Muslim home, the harem was the dwelling space designated for wives, concubines, and female relatives. Only family members and eunuchs were permitted in.

Over time, Shajara and al-Salih grew closer, and she eventually became his favourite concubine. He bestowed her the title Shajara al-Durr, which translates to "Tree of Pearls." Soon after, As-Salih Ayyub married her following the birth of their son. Tragically, they do not have any more children, and their son died in infancy. After ascending to the throne, As-Salih Ayyub trusted his wife to govern while he was on military missions. As she oversaw kingdom affairs, she had the authority to make decrees and, because of her understanding of her husband's military, she also had sway over the army.

Shajara's Kipchak heritage helped al-Salih enlist Mamluk (male Kipchak) soldiers. He first focused on regaining control of Egypt and winning everyone's allegiance within his direct sphere of influence.

The Role in the Seventh Crusade: A Strategic Victory

When Sultan As-Shalih led Egypt, a war between Muslims and Christians broke out. The Crusaders attacked Egypt from France. French forces launched a military campaign into Islamic territory. At that time, the Crusaders began to enter the territory of Dimyat and Mansuroh in Egypt. Amid war, Sultan As-Shalih suddenly died. However, to maintain political stability in Egypt, Shajar al-Dur hid the news of her husband's death. It was only after the Muslims had won and managed to repulse the French forces, Shajar al-Durr finally announced the news of her husband's death.

However, the Crusaders, who had by then gained reinforcements and were preparing to march to Cairo, eventually learnt of the Sultan's passing. The Egyptian army, under the leadership of al-Malik Baibars, eventually defeated the French forces after they attacked the Egyptian camp close to Mansurah and killed Fakhr al-Din. The French besieged

QUEENS OF POWER 37

the Crusader army inside Mansurah and killed most of the Knights Templar and several of their commanders.

After her husband's death was concealed for months, until his son Turan Shah returned, Shajar al-Durr was able to effectively negotiate peace with the Crusaders and govern the nation covertly. However, Turan Shah, lacking Mamluks' support, quickly made enemies. Aware of this, he started to replace senior officials and gave her instructions to turn over the late Sultan's assets as well as her own. When Shajar al-Durr realised how dangerous he was to her, she sought the Mamluks' assistance and had Turan Shah killed. With the support of her Mamluk army, Shajar al-Durr was now the Sultan of Egypt and the head of state.

Despite her brief reign, the Queen of Pearls left a lasting impression. As the first Mamluk ruler of Egypt, she established a dynasty that, until the Ottomans, would dominate the political landscape of the area. She was a fervent supporter of the arts and invented a new style of architecture that fused the design of Mamluk tombs with that of Islamic madrassas. This style of architecture persisted long after she left power, and the custom of affixing a tomb with a charitable donation, albeit in a modified form, is still practiced today.

Her mausoleum, an enduring tribute to her remarkable legacy, still stands proudly on al-Khalifa Street in the heart of Old Cairo. Inside is a Tree of Pearls, a complex mosaic design coated with gold and inlaid with mother of pearl. Shajar al-Durr, one of Egypt's greatest female monarchs and the Queen of Pearls, endures through her legacy.

The Fall of Shajar al-Durr: Political Intrigues and Death

Shajar al-Durr played a crucial role in the shift from the Ayyubid to the Mamluk era, serving as the wife of the final Ayyubid sultan, later as sultana, and ultimately as the first Mamluk sultan. After her husband's death on May 2, 1250, she governed until July, when she wed Izz al-Din Aybak and declared him sultan. Following an earlier sultana in India, she is thought to have been only the second female ruler in the history of Islam.

After the Crusaders were defeated and Louis IX sent back to France, Shajar al-Durr helped protect Cairo, Egypt, and Jerusalem. However, once she disclosed the sultan's passing, she encountered more difficulties. The Syrian emirs declined to acknowledge her rule. Conflicts with her new husband along with his other wives persisted until she was suspected of orchestrating his murder in a bathtub. Shajar al-Durr's subsequent marriage appeared more of a political move to stabilise the solution.

Tragically, the Tree of Pearls was found nude and battered to death (allegedly by wooden clogs) outside the Citadel in Cairo on April 28, 1257, and was promptly imprisoned.

Chapter Seven

Amina of Zazzau: The Warrior Queen of Nigeria

Although men have controlled many African dynasties, did you know that some amazing, remarkable, and inspirational women have also held leadership positions in their nations and tribes? Among such women is Amina, the Queen of Zazzau.

The modern city of Zaria, located in Kaduna State, Nigeria, is called Zazzau. Queen Amina of Zaria, also referred to as the Warrior Queen, was the first female to hold the position of Sarauniya (queen) in a culture that men controlled.

She was an accomplished Hausa warrior who led a sizable army that considerably enlarged her empire and conquered numerous lands.

Five portrayals of legendary founding personalities who, in one way or another, left a lasting impact for their countries are presented in African Roots, a DW series on individuals who influenced African history.

Pre-Colonial Hausa States: Zazzau's Significance

The Hausa States, also known as Hausa Bakwai or Hausaland, were an informal association of city-states (or kingdoms) in what is now northern Nigeria and Niger situated between the Niger River and Lake Chad. Despite their connections, the seven states—Biram, Daura, Gobir, Kano, Katsina, Rano, and Zaria (also known as Zazzau)—were distinct in that they never united under a single ruler.

Beyond the Jos plateau, the northern plains were home to the Hausa lands. These lands were the Trans-Saharan pathways to Northern Africa and the South and served as a crossroads accessible to the states of Mali, Songhai, and Bornu. As a result of this advantageous position, the Hausa regions saw a surge of foreigners, primarily traders and priests. This greatly influenced the politics of the various states.

The states mostly fought internal battles, although occasionally, they cooperated. However, from the 16th century until the early 19th century, when they were overrun and made emirates of the newly emerging Fulani Sokoto Caliphate following a holy war, they prospered together through trade and agriculture. In the following century, the annexation of the old emirates and Bornu formed the northern districts of the British Protectorate of Nigeria.

The Hausa mythology states that Bayajidda, a Muslim ruler from Baghdad, founded the kingdoms. After receiving a negative reception at the court of the ruler of the monarchy of Kanem, Bayajidda reportedly left for the city of Daura in the east. There, he married the Queen of Daura after slaying a gigantic serpent that had been causing them problems.

After giving birth to a seventh son (Bawogari) for Bayajidda, the Queen, who had previously had six sons, all seven went on to rule the seven kingdoms. Some historians think that East African immigrants may have built the republics, while others believe that Berber tribesmen from North Africa may have done so after mingling with native populations.

The Hausa people lived in the Sahel, which offered rich agricultural land. They also developed ingenious methods, such as fertiliser application and crop rotation, which strengthened their agricultural industry even further. The Hausa people's primary crops were millet, sorghum, maize, rice, peanuts, beans, henna, tobacco, and onions.

The Hausa States' strategic location allowed them to benefit from trade between West Africa, North Africa, and even the Middle East. They were neighbours of the Kingdom of Ghana, the Songhai Empire, and the powerful Mali Empire. Like most ancient African civilisations, the Hausa traded in kola nuts, salt, gold, ivory, leather, horses, animal hides, and slaves.

By the fourteenth century, Kano emerged as the preeminent Hausa state. As the hub of trade, culture, and education, Kano failed to impose its superior status on the other Hausa states, each of which battled for independence. The only person to surpass Kano in prominence was Katsina. However, Zaria enjoyed several conquests and even received tribute from Kano and Katsina, however briefly, under the great Queen Amina's reign.

Amina's Early Life: Shaping a Warrior Queen

Amina, who rose to become the head of the biggest Hausa tribe, was born in Zazzau, present-day Nigeria, in the sixteenth century. From an early age, she practiced fighting and won the military's esteem. Hausaland's core consists of the seven original states: Katsina, Daura, Gobir, Rano, Kano, Zazzau, and Garun Gabas.

Together, they cover an area of around 500 square miles. In the 16th century, Amina's mother, Queen Bakwa Turunku, constructed the capital city of Zazzau in Zaria, which bears her younger daughter's name. Zazzau was eventually renamed Zaria, which is now a region in modern-day Nigeria.

Trading in foreign metals, horses, cola, salt, cloth, and other goods made the family rich. Following her father's death in 1566, Amina's younger brother Karama was given the throne. Despite the calm and wealth that marked her father's reign, Amina decided to spend her time practicing her military talents with the Zazzau cavalry troops. As a result, she finally rose to prominence as the head of the Zazzau warriors, during which she amassed substantial money and received multiple military honours.

Military Campaigns: Expansion and Fortification

After her brother passed away, Amina ascended to the throne. After three months, she oversaw armies of more than 20,000 soldiers who enlarged Zazzau's realm to its greatest extent and established unobstructed trade routes. She also gave the Zazzau military metal helmets and body armour. As the first female ruler of an African state, she will live on in history. Many learning institutions bear her name in remembrance of the courageous and gifted leader, who passed away 34 years after ascending to the throne.

Zazzau was located at the intersection of three important northern African trade routes during Amina's rule, linking the Sahara with the isolated marketplaces of the southern woodland regions and the western Sudan. Throughout the 15th and 16th centuries, the Hausa people and their adjacent towns engaged in constant warfare due to the rise and fall of the Songhai, who were more powerful and dominant, and the ensuing struggle to control trade routes. The expansion of Zazzau beyond its original boundaries and the subjection of captured cities to vassal status were the two goals of her conquests.

The growth of Amina's kingdom ensured Zaria's prosperity by making it the trading hub for all of southern Hausaland, crossing the conventional east-to-west trans-Saharan axis. According to one account, Amina brought unprecedented wealth to the land, including 10,000 kola nuts and 40 eunuchs as a tribute payment. "She used money, slaves, and new crops to increase the wealth and power of her empire."

Amina is recognised as the architect who designed the city's sturdy mud walls, which served as the model for the defences found in every Hausa state. She surrounded numerous conquered cities with many of these defences, which came to be identified as Ganuwar, Amina or Amina's walls.

During the Fulani jihad, the Fulani took control of the area by 1805. British soldiers took Zaria as a protectorate state under Frederick Lugard in 1901. According to reports, Zaria requested British protection against Kontagora slave raids in the same year. The British deprived the emirate of the majority of its vassal states in 1902 after a Zaria magaji (indicative) killed British Captain Moloney at Keffi.

Zaria has been one of Nigeria's biggest traditional emirates since the country gained independence from the British in 1960. The emirs maintain the conventional leadership of the former kingdom-states and wield considerable power in the region, even as nation-states emerge in Africa.

The Myth and Reality of Queen Amina's Legacy

There are others who contend that Amina never existed and that her story is a myth. Nonetheless, there is proof that she exists. The walls she erected around the important cities she overran serve as one illustration. In Zaria, there are also still buildings and remnants of her castle and military training grounds.

There are rumours that her other siblings' direct descendants still live and belong to the emirate's elite governing dynasties, even though she never had children of her own. Although her cause and location of death are still up for debate, it is generally agreed that she was killed in combat at Atagara, which is located in modern-day Kogi State in north central Nigeria.

Legend has it that she took a man from the enemy after a fight, spent the night with him, and then killed him the following day so he could not spread any gossip. She never married, maybe following in the footsteps of Queen Elizabeth I of England and had no children. Before she passed away, Amina ruled for 34 years. The folklore states that she was murdered during a military operation close to Bida, Nigeria. A monument of Amina can be found at the National Arts Theatre in Lagos State.

Chapter Eight

Arwa al-Sulayhi: The Queen of Yemen

Sayyida Hurra Queen Arwa, a member of Yemen's Isma'ili Sulayhid dynasty (eleventh–twelfth century), was a remarkable Muslim female leader who concurrently possessed both political and spiritual power. Before her death, she ruled Yemen as a queen consort working with her husband, her son's regent, and an independent sovereign.

She exhibited self-assurance and took decisive action to protect her throne, whether against dissident family members or enemies of her realm. She provided justice and prosperity to her people while holding the fiercely competitive and strong Yemeni tribal elders in control. Did Yemen suffer as a result of her rule? Apparently not! She was referred to as "their Mistress" and was immensely popular. Let's explore!

The Assassination of al-Amir and the Rise of Tayyibi Isma'ilism

In October 1130, a Nizari from a rival Isma'ili party killed the tenth Isma'ili Fatimid imam-caliph, al-Amir biAhkam Allah, in Cairo. The Nizari believed that the rightful claim to the dynasty had been usurped about 35 years earlier. A few months before his assassination, al-Amir wrote an official letter (sijill) to Sayyida Hurra, Queen Arwa of Yemen, announcing the birth of his child and legitimate heir, Abu'l Qasim al-Tayyib. This news brought great joy to the community.

However, in the political turmoil that followed the assassination of the imam-caliph in Cairo, the child "disappeared," never to be seen again. In reaction to the succession issue, Queen Arwa quickly and firmly proclaimed the missing infant al-Tayyib as the rightful heir of the deceased imam-caliph al-Amir.

By creating the new role of "supreme missionary" (da'i mutlaq) to safeguard the recently formed Tayyibi Isma'ili mission, she thereby built the foundation for Tayyibi Isma'ilism and strengthened it. She could do so because she was a hujja, or spiritual leader, the second-highest ranking figure in the Isma'ili religious hierarchy after the imam. The queen's timely intervention in the ongoing Fatimid succession struggle changed the course of history.

Hurra Sayyida Yemen's Isma'ili Sulayhid dynasty's Queen Arwa is among the most remarkable and politically savvy Muslim female rulers. Because she simultaneously possessed both governmental and spiritual authority, her sovereignty is unique.

Were it not for the fortunate discovery of some Tayyibi Isma'ili sources—hidden for centuries by scholarly elites, mainly out of fear of persecution—the significant role she played in the succession, preservation, and extension of the Tayyibi Isma'ili group might have remained unknown.

Biographers and historians universally praise the brilliance, political acumen, and charisma of Queen Arwa. In one case, for instance, the Queen is described as "well-read and, in addition to the talent of writing, [she] possessed a retentive memory loaded with the chronology of past time."

Nothing could compare to the interlinear glosses she had placed in her own handwriting in the pages of books she had read, both in terms of language construction and meaning. This queen was undoubtedly a highly accomplished writer. One historian describes her as a woman of flawless wisdom and erudition, surpassing men even and far exceeding women who remained confined to their rooms. Another describes her as a woman of tremendous devotion, integrity, and perfection.

Although she had de facto political power for seventy-one years, Queen Arwa effectively ruled Yemen for 54 years. She first served as a queen consort with her spouse al-Mukarram bi Allah (1067–1084), then as her son's queen regent (1084–1094), and finally as a sovereign in her own right until her death in 1138. The war of succession, the decline of the Fatimid dynasty in Egypt, and the increasing economic, political, and spiritual influence of the Sulayhid Queen Arwa all occurred simultaneously. But in the end, her passing essentially ended the Sulayhid dynasty.

Three consecutive Fatimid imam-caliphs in Cairo, beginning with al-Mustansir Billah (1029–1094), were intimately linked to her authority in Yemen. Her ability to maintain loyalty to the Fatimid imam-caliphs in Cairo while preserving a degree of administrative autonomy in Yemen is what sets her apart as an experienced politician.

Arwa was born in 1047 (or 1048) to Ahmad b. Ja'far b. Musa al-Sulayhi and al-Radah bint al-Fari b. Musa. Amir b. Sulayiman al-Zawahi, the son of a former da'i (Isma'ili preacher and member of an allied tribe, became a political competitor of his stepdaughter, Queen Arwa, after Radah's husband passed away (no date is specified). After her father's death, young Arwa moved in with her maternal uncle, 'Ali b. Muhammad al-Sulayhi.

An ardent advocate of the Fatimids in Egypt, 'Ali b. Muhammad al-Sulayhi later fortified the da'wa in Yemen, making it one of the Fatimid dynasty's most vital commercial and geopolitical strongholds along the Indian Ocean coast. Asma bint Shihab, the wife of Arwa's paternal uncle and another strong Isma'ili woman in both intellect and politics, raised Arwa. A close friend and relative to her husband, Asma worked alongside him in the administration and control of the state.

In 1066, Arwa wed her paternal cousin, al-Mukarram b. 'Ali. Her uncle/father-in-law thought so highly of the new bride that he gave her the port city of Aden's yearly revenue as a bride price. But after his older brother, the heir apparent, died prematurely, Al-Mukarram was suddenly thrown into the political spotlight. Unfortunately, 'Ali suffered defeat and was beheaded, and the women who were with him, including his wife Asma, were captured. The severed heads of 'Ali b. Muhammad and his younger brother were displayed to the imprisoned women at a stronghold.

One day, Arwa reportedly explained to her aunt Asma that she had a dream in which she "swept the king's palace." Upon hearing this, Asma said, "It seems like I shared my vision... By Allah!". The royal couple sought to provide young Arwa the greatest education and training possible after recognising her talent and intelligence early on.

By passing a loaf of bread to a vagrant through her chained window, Asma was able to sneak the news of her whereabouts and alert her son of her imprisonment. Al-Mukarram swiftly launched an assault on the stronghold, rescuing his mother and her friends and directing the removal of his father's and uncle's severed heads.

Al-Mukarram was the king and da'i of the Isma'ili Sulayhids, succeeding his father in both roles. Due to his prominent status, his wife Arwa became increasingly involved in governmental issues. Nonetheless, Queen Mother Asma remained in charge of all governmental and financial activities, controlled key strategic intelligence, and oversaw political affairs and governance.

Queen Mother Asma remained the de facto ruler of the state's affairs until her death in 1074–1075. According to Husain Hamdani, the Sulayhids were extremely lucky to have had two notable ladies who significantly influenced their husbands' careers and the governance of the state.

Given their close friendship and how easily Arwa took over for her mother-in-law following her death, Asma merely observed Arwa helping her with numerous official responsibilities. The life of Yemen's Great the monarch, the Sayyida Hurra, also known as "The noble lady who is liberated and independent," began when Arwa was thrust into the political spotlight following the death of her mother-in-law and the paralysis of her husband. Because he "honoured the counsel of his spouse and had great trust in her intelligence and intelligence," al-Mukarram personally invited her to assume state leadership.

Umara seemed uncomfortable with this reversal of gender roles—not so much because he doubted Arwa's political abilities, but because he struggled to explain it within the cultural framework of his time. Arwa was a young, attractive woman, and Umara struggled to reconcile her desirability with her political authority. Umara depicts her as pleading with her husband for "personal freedom" rather than the burdens of governance.

The queen "assigned her husband his residential role, while she enthusiastically took up the duties of running the government in times of turmoil that synchronised with her rulership." Arwa swiftly established her power by reversing their roles.

The young queen petitioned the Fatimid imam-caliph al-Mustansir in Egypt through a sijill, to appoint a new da'i in India. In 1075, Imam al-Mustansir granted the Queen authority over the da'wa in India, affirming her jurisdiction over both Oman's and India's affairs.

Early in her reign, Arwa made the wise political choice to relocate her capital from San'a to Dhu Jibla in central Yemen. The decision was ostensibly justified by al-Mukarram's health, but it was actually motivated by the fact that San'a was turning into a rebellious hotspot that was challenging the Sulayhids' authority and by extension, Arwa's rule. In a display of power, the wise queen rode to Dhu Jibla at the head of a sizable army to survey the location of her new home. Everyone "gathered around Sayiddah's stirrup, acknowledging her authority" there.

She requested that her husband report on what he observed people carrying in San'a and Dhu Jibla from the palace windows. He observed individuals with drawn swords and other weapons in San'a, and "vessels filled with ghee or with honey" in Dhu Jibla. The queen assured her husband that it was much better to live among these hard-working people. Therefore, they moved the seat of government from San'a to Dhu Jibla in 1074.

In actuality, Queen Arwa was the legitimate ruler and head of state, even if her spouse was the king and she was the force behind his throne. However, in accordance with custom, the Queen had her husband, the official head of state, have khutbas chanted in his name.

Arwa's involvement in state issues increased as her royal spouse withdrew farther into the palace's interior. Tribal rivalries, hostilities, and the struggle for global dominance were heightened by her gender and prominence, which also contributed to the resurgence of long-standing disputes. Queen Arwa set out to put down several uprisings, surrounded by a small group of devoted allies and counsellors. She set up a cunning trap since she was especially determined to exact revenge for the horrific decapitation of her uncle/father-in-law.

Taking advantage of the local views on gender roles, the Queen gave one of her supporters instructions to inform Sa'id al-Ahwal (Sa'id the Squint-Eyed), the chief of the Najahid tribe, that she was in charge of the government because her husband was paralysed. This flattery was meant to feed Sa'id's ambitions, making him believe he was "the most powerful king in Yemen."

Meanwhile in Cairo, the Fatimid imam-caliph al-Mustansir—Arwa's overlord—was enmeshed in ethnic disputes. A grand-nephew of the fierce and vivacious princess Sitt al-Mulk, he found himself caught between ethnic conflicts within his court. His mother, Rasad, an African concubine of the seventh Fatimid imam-caliph, al-Zahir wielded considerable influence. Despite having a large number of slaves and concubines of many races, ethnicities, and religions, many of the Fatimid caliphs chose not to get married.

When his father passed away in 1036, al-Mustansir was just six or seven years old, which propelled him to become the eighth Fatimid imam-caliph and a position of power in politics and religion. After the young imam's influential wazir died in 1044–1045, Rasad rose to prominence. She took over right away and held onto all political authority, essentially continuing to serve as queen regent for "a long period of time."

Rasad, the so-called evil genius of al-Mustansir's reign, is said to have stoked the ethnic hostility between Turks, Arabs, and Africans, leaving the state's treasury empty and the warriors worn out. Although this story is debatable, Rasad fled to Baghdad with her children in 1069 after the Turks ultimately defeated the black slaves. In any event, she had much less authority and sway inside the royal court.

Al-Mukarram passed away in 1084 after a protracted illness, but the wise Queen Arwa concealed her husband's passing for nearly a year. Any time a ruler's succession was to take place right after his or her death, the transition tended to cause a crisis. The queen correctly believed that some ambitious local leaders may attempt to overthrow her and that her society could be ripped apart, just as it had been following the assassination of her father-in-law. As a result, she waited for imam-caliph al-Mustansir to give her the sijill, or formal letter.

Upon learning of al-Mukarram's passing, the Queen chose her son, al-Mukarram al-Asghar, also known as "the Younger," as the heir apparent and successor to the Yemeni da'wa. To ensure a smooth transition of power, the imam-caliph instructed the Queen "to act in her son's interest and to assist him to obtain the loyalty of the other members of the da'wa in Yemen."

Given the young heir's age and the potential for chaos, the imam-caliph felt compelled to strengthen the Queen's hold on power by giving the Yemenites the order to submit to the Queen or risk "rejection as infidels, with the rage of God, the Prophet, and the imams falling upon them."

In a move that has never been seen before, the imam-caliph then appointed Queen Arwa as the hujja of Yemen and India—the second-highest position to the imam in the Isma'ili spiritual hierarchy. As a hujja, "Arwa became the figure of faith whose example the community of believers were to follow." In the Muslim world, no other woman has ever held the dual positions of state and religious establishment leadership like Queen Arwa.

The da'wa elite had persuaded him that Queen Arwa, "the Lady, the Righteous, the Faithful, the Strong, the Preserver of Religion... the Supporter of the adherents, the Cave of the followers... the Supporter of the Head of the Faithful and the Guardian of the Blessed Followers," had absorbed the imam's knowledge and expertise.

Umara, a historian from the twelfth century, wavered between opinions about the scope of Queen Arwa's spiritual authority and the governing body of the imam-caliph's order. However, the Idris of the fifteenth century, also a Tayyibi da'i mutlaq, had no qualms about accepting the Queen's spiritual authority and the imam's ruling as final. Because of the kinds of tasks given to her, Arwa, however, saw the imam-caliph's behaviour as political rather than religious.

In her dual role, Queen Arwa oversaw the state's affairs with her newly extended spiritual authority. On paper, however, the da'i Lamak b. Malik controlled the da'wa administration, while her son al-Mukarram al-Asghar was in state command. She appointed her cousin, da'i Saba b. Ahmad al-Sulayhi, as head of state security, entrusting him with a significant role in the da'wa and the education of her sons.

Some tribe chiefs, including a few of her own allies, believed she would not be able to maintain her rigorous administrative role because she was a younger widow with little children. Some saw this period of change as a chance to question the Queen's rule, attempting to depose her and seize power in the Sulayhid state.

In 1086, one of the state's longstanding foes decisively defeated da'i Saba. Angered by this failure, Queen Arwa's stepfather, Amir b. Sulayman al-Zawahi rebelled against both Saba and the Queen, launching a rebellion. Faced with this crisis, Queen Arwa wrote to the imam-caliph in Cairo to ask for his support while the two leaders were engaged in combat.

However, both of the Queen's possible opponents passed away in a short period of time: Amir b. Sulayman died the year after, while da'i Saba al-Sulayhi died in 1097–1098. The queen outlived both of them and, after a close encounter with her cousin da'i Saba, was free of significant political disputes within her clan.

The queen had to ward off male relatives, rivals, and tribal adversaries in a variety of contexts including internal strife and challenges to her governmental authority. She also had to vigorously defend her autonomy and honour in areas where she might be vulnerable, like as marriage and sexuality. In the years after her husband's passing, three events put her will to maintain her independence and her capacity to handle the constant political and personal threats to her power to the test.

Queen Arwa, a young widow, was arguably the most desirable woman in her era. Women were frequently sought after and remarried shortly following a husband's death because widowhood was not stigmatised, especially among the aristocracy. In many contemporary Muslim countries, widowhood is viewed as unlucky, which is very different from the social status of widows in the early days of Islam.

Yet, despite the political and social pressures surrounding her, she remained independent and firmly in control. The stage was perfectly set. Her palace was filled with standing ministers, staff members, and even a Fatimid state official.

From a practical standpoint, it appears that the imam-caliphs in Cairo were unable to challenge her rule. Having already been proclaimed a hujja, obedience was due to her, and she was "immensely popular" with her people. In fact, she had become commercially, politically, and religiously indispensable to the Egyptian leadership. The Queen

Arwa, also known as Sayyida Hurra, outlived three succeeding Fatimid imam-caliphs and held onto her throne for an additional 44 years.

After her husband, al-Mukarram, died, Arwa placed Mufaddal in command of a campaign against some rebellious tribes and sent him to the fortress of al-Takar, where she spent her summers. A gang of Shafi'i jurists overthrew the Queen and occupied the stronghold while al-Mufaddal was away. Then, al-Mufaddal hurried to al-Takar and besieged it right away. The rebel jurist commander responded by ordering al-Mufaddal's concubines to dress in their finest attire, climb onto the fortress' top, and play their tambourines—an uncommon form of retaliation. Al-Mufaddal gazed in horror as his harem's women danced in front of the people.

Disgraced, a dejected al-Mufaddal killed himself in a fit of jealousy. When al-Mufaddal died, the Queen simultaneously sued for diplomacy and led her troops to a location close to the Dhu Jibla castle. She provided the jurists a compromise and was "very scrupulous in ensuring the compliance of treaty obligations."

The queen kept her word to ensure the security of their lives and property when they yielded to her power and gave her back control of the stronghold. Queen Arwa's abilities to maintain her rule, discipline her subjects, and resolve challenges related to her political authority are all demonstrated by these three instances, as well as probably others for which there are no written records.

Known for promoting harmony, peace, and prosperity, Queen's Arwa's capable leadership won her a great deal of admiration and respect; one poet even said that she had done for Yemen what other kings had failed to do. Her diplomatic and strategic leadership fostered economic growth, particularly in the infrastructure and agricultural sectors. The fact that her name is spoken in the khutba sermons, a rare honour, highlights her exceptional status among Muslim rulers and solidifies her status as the first regent queen in the Islamic world.

At just 17 years old, Arwa married her cousin, Ahmad al-Mukarram bin Ali bin Muhammad al-Sulayhi, in 1066, receiving the city of Aden as her mahr. Her mother-in-law, Queen Asma, played a significant role in her early political life. After the death of her husband, Arwa worked closely with both her husband and Queen Asma to grow Yemen.

Although Ahmad, Arwa's husband, succeeded Sayyid Ali al-Sulayhi as king, he was bedridden and paralysed. To demonstrate her dominance, he granted Arwa all of his authority, and the khutbah included her name right after the title of the Fatimid Caliph, al-Mustansir Billah.

Moving the capital from Sana'a to Jibla was one of her first moves to better position herself to overthrow Sa'id ibn Najar of Zabīd, the Najahid monarch. She did that to exact revenge for the murder of her father-in-law. She could do this by tricking him into falling into a trap. At Jibla, she constructed a new palace and converted the old one into a magnificent mosque, where she was ultimately laid to rest.

Administrative Reforms and Religious Patronage

Significant public welfare and infrastructure advancements were hallmarks of Queen Arwa's reign. To provide her subjects with access to clean water, she invested a lot of time and money in building mosques, hospitals, dams, and reservoirs. Her business, industrial, and agricultural endeavours produced thriving enterprises, including the development of the cotton, wool, and silk sectors.

She also improved women's social status while in power by defending their rights. Her legacy as an emperor who put her people's safety and well-being first was further cemented by her extraordinary war planning skills and diplomatic savvy. She was given the title Bilqis al-Sughra, an allusion to the fabled Queen of Sheba, and her reign is still revered and adored by Yemenis today. It is frequently referred to as Yemen's golden period.

Arwa's Influence in the Ismaili Muslim Community

The Imams bestowed upon her the greatest honours and titles in acknowledgement of her brilliance and dedication, a testament to her high standing and the important tasks she was given. She was tasked by the Imams to supervise the daʿwa of al-Hind and al-Sind in addition to Yemen. The Fatimi daʿwa combined these areas, which were already linked by trade.

The growth of the Bohra community in various areas demonstrates the importance of this relationship. Particularly following the fall of the Fatimi Empire, her leadership was essential to the Fatimi Tayyibi daʿwa's survival.

Arwa improved the route from the city to Samarra and expanded the majestic mosque in Sana'a. She commissioned the construction of Queen Arwa's new castle and namesake mosque in Jibla. She is also recognised for building many schools within her territory. Arwa improved the economy by being interested in advancing agriculture. Her reign served as a template for many later leaders since she was a woman who could exercise political power while also showing empathy and concern for her followers.

To prepare for the satr of the 21st Fatimi Imam al-Tayyib, the 20th Imam al-Amir tasked Queen Arwa with establishing the office of al-Dai al-Mutlaq. She appointed Syedna Zu'aib bin Musa as the first al-Dai al-Mutlaq in Yemen, forming the foundation of the Dawoodi Bohra community.

After nearly seven decades of remarkable governance, Queen Arwa passed away in 1138 at 90, leaving a legacy of devotion to Imam al-Tayyib. Her will, gifting her jewels to the 21st Imam, and her spiritual contributions are honoured by the Dawoodi Bohras, who revere her as the mother of the Tayyibi dāʿis.

Chapter Nine

Zaynab Al-Nafzawiyyat: The Influential Consort

Although Zaynab al-Nafzawiya's life story is not entirely clear, she was born to Ishaq al-Houari in the early 11th century in Aghmat, which is now part of Morocco or Maghreb, the region's main commercial and cultural hub. She was a concubine of Sheikh Yusuf ibn Ouatas, the head of the Aghmats, before marrying Laggut, the final ruler of the Aghmats. Being politically astute, Zaynab knew who to support and when.

One of those women, Zaynab al-Nafzawiya, used her two greatest weapons—beauty and wit—to maliciously challenge patriarchal control. The nomadic tribes of Lamthuna and Gudala, who came from the middle of the desert, were waging the first battles to seize power as the Idrissid dynasty gradually ceded its basis of authority. The most influential rulers in the Almoravid dynasty were susceptible to the enchantment of the fabled Zaynab al-Nafzawiya.

The Almoravid Dynasty: Origins and Expansion

The Almoravid dynasty, which ruled for a century over an empire spanning from the eastern borders of the Maghreb to Andalusia, originated from a nomadic clan that was indigenous to the Sahara.

The Almoravids gave Morocco its name by founding Marrakech, the country's second imperial metropolis after Fès. Among the many architectural wonders of this period are the Almoravid Qoubba in Marrakech, the Grand Mosque of Tlemcen, the mausoleum of the Abbadid monarch of Seville, and Al Mutamid ibn Abbad in Aghmat (30 km from Marrakech, at the base of the High Atlas).

One man, Abdallah ibn Yasin, was largely responsible for the establishment of the Almoravid Dynasty. Ibn Yasin lived in Waggag ibn Zelu's ribat, which means "fortification" at Arabic. He encountered Yahya ibn Ibrahim, a chieftain who felt that conservative rituals were being abandoned and was looking for a Malliki teacher for his people. After being radicalised by Ibn Ibrahim, Ibn Yasin began converting others to his beliefs and advocating for the overthrow of the present administration.

Three primary factions controlled the Maghreb and al-Andalus region at the time: the Zenata controlled the north, the Masmuda controlled central Morocco, and the Sanhaja were concentrated in two main areas: the Eastern Hills of the Maghreb and the Western Sahara.

Ibn Yasin aimed to unify the Berber Muslims under a single cause, rallying them to his vision of religious unity and reform. He turned to the Lamtuna tribe, where he gained substantial support. Drawing followers to his interpretation of the Quran, he emphasised the necessity of adhering to a stringent form of Islam. Through recounting tales from the early life of Prophet Muhammad, Ibn Yasin advocated for military campaigns and conquest to ensure strict adherence to Islamic principles.

At the time, three primary factions controlled the Maghreb and al-Andalus region: the Zenata controlled the north, the Masmuda dominated central Morocco, and the Sanhaja were centered in two main areas. He added that eliminating resistance to God's law was just as important as abiding by it.

Ibn Yasin believed that anything and everyone that did not follow Islamic law may be considered "the enemy." In particular, he viewed the Berber custom of tribalism as a significant obstacle to establishing a unified empire. If the Muslim tribes were to be formed into a strong whole, he thought they all needed to be brought together.

The Lamtuna leadership saw Ibn Yasin's new philosophy as a great fit with their long-standing objective of regaining their lost lands and reforming the Sanhaja union. In the middle of the 11th century, approximately 1051, the Lamtuna—led by Abdallah ibn Yasin and Yahya ibn Umar—began calling themselves the al-Murabitin, or the Almoravids.

With his followers united, Ibn Yasin set out to expand his influence and lay the foundation for his empire. In 1053, the Almoravids launched their first campaign, spreading the teachings of their leader. They approached the Sanhaja Berber tribes in North Africa, gaining their allegiance and securing control over a critical portion of the Trans-Saharan trade route.

This key economic and strategic asset provided a steady flow of wealth and significant leverage. Building on this momentum, they captured Sijilmasa to the north in 1054 and Aoudaghost to the south in 1055, solidifying their dominance over this vital trade network.

As a result, the Almoravids gained total control over the West and North African portions of the Trans-Saharan trade routes. Nearly all of northern and eastern Africa was connected to Europe and Asia via this route, making it the most important trading route in the world. At its height of popularity, this route carried more than half of all global trade.

Not long after their campaigns began, Yahya ibn Umar fell in battle, paving the way for Ibn Yasin's brother, Abu Bakr ibn Umar, to assume leadership of the Almoravids. Meanwhile, Abdallah ibn Yasin rose to prominence as the spiritual leader of the movement, wielding immense influence over the growing empire.

Together, the brothers accelerated the expansion of the Almoravid Dynasty across North Africa. Their conquests eventually brought them into conflict with the Berghouata, a group labeled "heretics." In 1059, during a battle near the village of Krifla, close to Rommani, Morocco, Abdallah ibn Yasin was killed. Despite his death, he left behind a formidable empire that continued to shape the region.

Zaynab's Background: Wealth to Power

Zaynab al-Nafzawiya was a prominent and influential woman from North Africa during the 11th century, renowned for her intelligence, beauty, and political acumen. She played a significant role in establishing and consolidating the Almoravid dynasty, which ruled large parts of the Maghreb and al-Andalus. Zaynab was born into the Nafzawa tribe, a Berber group from present-day Tunisia. Her prosperous and culturally rich upbringing likely contributed to her development as an intelligent and independent woman. She was known for her exceptional beauty, charisma, and keen business sense, particularly in trade and finance.

The Role of Zaynab in Yusuf ibn Tashfin's Rule

According to some accounts, he was an Almoravid king and conqueror from North Africa who established the first Berber Empire, which brought Spain and North Africa together. After conquering Morocco, Yusuf ibn Tashfin (also spelt Tashufin) established Marrakesh as the capital of the Almoravid, a recently formed Islamic empire in North Africa.

In 1061, his cousin Abu Bakr appointed Tashfin commander of the Almoravid army in Morocco. This enabled Abu Bakr, the Almoravids' leader at the time, to drive south into the desert and quell a tribal uprising. After returning home and realising that Tashfin had performed his commander's duties in an honourable manner, Abu Bakr gave over his authority and even his wife to Tashfin. By 1063, Tashfin had captured the cities controlled by the Zenata Berbers in central Morocco. In 1069, he conquered Fez, Morocco.

Al-Muizz Billah and Fadl were the two children Zaynab entrusted to Yusuf ibn Tashfin, the monarch of the Almoravid Empire, after their marriage in 1071. She gave Yusuf advice and her negotiation skills helped him conquer Maghreb. For this reason, she was known as "The Magician," and many believed she possessed supernatural abilities and could speak with genies. Although her exact year of death is unknown, it is thought to have occurred in 1075 or later. She significantly impacted Berber women in the future, allowing royal ladies to participate in politics and education and removing the veil requirement imposed by Zaynab.

Zaynab's Legacy: Influence Beyond the Throne

The most influential rulers in the Almoravid dynasty were susceptible to the enchantment of the fabled Zaynab al-Nafzawiya. Her political knowledge and intelligence further increased her attraction. In addition to her unrivalled beauty, Zaynab al-Nafzawiya was commended for her governance abilities.

Historians note that Zaynab al-Nafzawiya had a significant impact on decision-making, particularly in the area of public affairs, despite the fact that many women at the period lived in the shadow of their husbands. Women were comparatively free in public life throughout the Almoravid era. They occupied a significant position in society because they were trusted with domestic rule.

Chapter Ten

Queen Aisha Al-Hurra: The Last Muslim Queen of Granada

Born in 1485, Sayyida al-Hurra—whose name at birth is unknown—was a noblewoman whose title means "Noble Lady." She was the daughter of Chefchaouen's emir, Ali ibn Rashid, who lived in what is now northwest Morocco.

After her husband, Prince Ali al-Mandri, passed away, Sayyida al-Hurra famously took over as governor of Tétouan, situated in the same region. She was profoundly impacted by her childhood exile from the Kingdom of Grenada, which the Spanish retook, and she would go on to lead missions against the Portuguese colonists in Ceuta. As a result, she gained notoriety as the Muslim "pirate queen."

The Nasrid Dynasty and the Fall of Granada

The Emirate of Granada was ruled by the Arab Nasrid dynasty from 1232 to 1492. It was the Iberian Peninsula's final Muslim dynasty. From Muhammad I's establishment of the dynasty in 1232 to Muhammad XII's surrender of all domains to Isabella I of Castile in 1492, Granada was governed by 23 sultans.

Muhammad I of Granada established a dynasty that ruled over Granada, Jaén, Almería, and Málaga. During the Reconquista campaigns, Christians overran Valencia, Játiva, and Jaén, and starting in 1243, the Nasrids were largely reduced to tribute-paying vassals. Granada remained an Islamic cultural hub. Later, the Nasrids forged partnerships with Morocco's Marinids.

The Nasrids are renowned for their palace construction during the 14th century, such as the Alhambra, which resulted from Ismail I and Muhammad V's labours. Using techniques from the 9th century in Baghdad, Nasrid crafts including ceramic overglaze and textile work were employed to create lusterware, initially in Málaga, Murcia, and Almería, and then in Manises by the 15th century. The subsequent form of colourful, glazed Italian ceramics termed maiolica was influenced by this pottery, first made under Muslim patronage before becoming Christian.

The Christian kingdoms of Castile and Aragon were united in 1469 when Ferdinand II of Aragon married Isabella I of Castile. The monarchs' joint goal was to conquer the final Muslim state on the Iberian Peninsula. At the same time, the Nasrids were fighting a civil war over the throne of Granada, and the Christians were beginning an offensive against the Emirate of Granada that would essentially end the Nasrid dynasty.

Abu l-Hasan Ali, the Sultan of Granada, was overthrown by his son Muhammad XII in the late 15th century. This sparked a bloody civil war in which rival factions fought for control. As internal conflict undermined the Muslim monarchy, Abu l-Hasan Ali sought safety in Málaga.

Christian soldiers seized the opportunity and stepped up their efforts, taking control of important Muslim areas. In 1483, Muhammad XII was taken prisoner at a battle at Lucena in Córdoba. At a crucial juncture in the Christian reconquest of Spain, he was released on the promise of allegiance to Isabella I of Castile and Ferdinand II of Aragon.

A conflict of authority with Muhammad XII persisted when Abu l-Hasan Ali ultimately abdicated in favour of his brother Muhammad XIII, Ruler of Granada, also known as Al-Zaghal (the courageous). Al-Zaghal lost the internal conflict but had to surrender to the Christians. In 1492, in exchange for financial rewards from the Spanish crown, Muhammad XII left the Iberian Peninsula, giving up Granada to Ferdinand and Isabella and receiving a dominion in the Alpujarras mountains. The status of mudéjar was granted to the remnant Muslim people.

The combined forces of Aragon and Castile (later united as Spain) overran the army of the Taifa Muslim kingdom of Granada and took the city at the Battle of Granada. The loss of Granada, the final bastion of Moorish sovereignty in Spain, ended 780 years of Muslim dominance over the Spanish peninsula, hence this very minor campaign had significant ramifications.

The Reconquista, a siege of the Christian nations of mediaeval Spain to expel the Moors, ended with the fall of Granada. Following this, Jews and Muslims were expelled from Spain, while some managed to stay by becoming Christians. Some of these, referred to as Moriscos and Morranos, continued to be covertly Jewish or Muslim. Regardless of how sincere their conversion was, many were the target of the Spanish Inquisition's suspicions and interrogations. Converts' descendants were likewise banished in 1609.

Later in the year of Granada's loss, Christopher Columbus set sail for the New World because of the Spanish and Portuguese desire to conquer other countries and their innate superiority complex towards the civilisations and religions they discovered there. Conveniencia, the Spanish word for the richness and constructive cultural interaction of Moorish Spain before 1492, may offer hints about how modern multi-cultural civilisations might handle the difficulties of diversity and peaceful coexistence.

Aisha al-Hurra's Life: From Nobility to Leadership

She was a member of the Wattasid dynasty and the second wife of the Moroccan king Abu al-Abbas Ahmad ibn Muhammad. Others say she is "one of the most significant female figures of the Islamic Civilisation in the modern age."

The Ottoman Empire had overrun Constantinople in 1453, bringing an end to the Eastern Byzantine Kingdom; the Portuguese Empire had started capturing ports along the western Moroccan coast in 1487; and the Reconquista had returned the peninsula of Iberia to European Christian rule by 1492, which ultimately resulted in the expulsion or compelled faith of Muslims in Spain. These events largely characterised the period of her life and career.

After the death of her first husband, Sidi al-Mandri II, who ruled Tétouan, in 1515, she emerged as the last person in Muslim history to claim the title "al-Hurra" in fact. Because al-Hurra refused to leave Tétouan, her marriage to her second husband is the only instance in Moroccan history of a king getting married outside of the capital city of Fez. After the Reconquista, a famous Muslim family of Andalusian nobility who had been banished to Morocco following the fall of Granada moved to Chefchaouen, where Sayyida al Hurra was born sometime between 1491 and 1495.

Lalla Zohra Fernandez, from Vejer de la Frontera, close to Cadiz, and Ali ibn Rashid al-Alami, the proprietor and emir of Chefchaouen, were her parents. She was a Sharifian and descended from Hasan ibn Ali via the Moroccan Sufi saint Abd al-Salam ibn Mashish al-Alami.

Sayyida had a joyful and safe childhood and spoke numerous languages fluently, including Portuguese and Castilian Spanish. Among her multiple tutors was the renowned Moroccan scholar Abdallah al-Ghazwani. At sixteen, she married Sidi al-Mandri II, a man thirty years her senior. He was the grandson or nephew of Ali al-Mandri, a companion of her father who had founded and served as governor of

Tétouan. He was also an Andalusian Moorish refugee. When she was still a child, she committed to her spouse.

Along with overseeing military operations and city defence, she also made important decisions with the help of advisors like her sibling, Ibrahim ben Rashid, a minister in Sultan al-Wattasi's administration in Fez. Although al-Hurra initially drew authority from her brother and husband, she had her own unique policies.

By working with the Ottoman corsair Barbarossa, she enabled his ships to make port calls in Morocco. The aim was to gain a strong ally in the fight to counter the Iberian threat. Additionally, she provided them with a market for the money they earned from hacking. As Risouni stated in the interview, the Ottomans were defending Algeria against Spain at the time.

In her homeland, al-Hurra was hailed as a hero for protecting the North from outside dangers. Although she was frequently referred to as a "pirate queen" in Europe, the Qasbah Museum refers to her as a "princess of jihad."

Muslim nations saw using pirates to attack European cities and ships as a means of retaliating against the forced exodus of Andalusi Muslims during the Spanish conquest of Granada. Piracy was thus viewed as a component of a religious duty to defend Muslim territories, grounded in Quranic precepts. On the other hand, European nations had a less favourable opinion of these activities.

Al-Hurra had to defend her land and keep the Europeans from taking it. She ran both aggressive and defensive campaigns to achieve this aim. To further her interests, such as selling European enslaved into slavery or capturing them back to their home countries, she used her personal forces and those she sponsored to attack multiple European cities and ships, capturing thousands of prisoners along with the ships and cargo.

For instance, her ships seized Portundo, a Portuguese man known as the prince of the sea, in 1528. Piracy provided al-Hurra with income and allowed them to improve their diplomatic ties with other nations.

The Siege of Granada: Aisha's Role and Resistance

The city of Granada was under siege during the Battle of Granada. The conflict lasted for several months before Granada gave up. Following several days of intense combat, Queen Isabella of Castile's royal imperial soldiers advanced into Granada and overthrew its final Muslim monarch, Muhammad XII.

Muhammad had been invited to the Queen's and her imperial armies' royal tent after the city was taken, where an official surrender was made. Following his surrender, Queen Isabella commanded Muhammad to depart from the Iberian Peninsula and travel to North Africa, where he was banished with the other Andalusian Muslims.

Aisha bin Muhammad was the final Muslim queen of Granada. She was a politically engaged monarch who significantly impacted state matters in the final years of the Emirate of Granada. No Arab woman has ever worked as hard as Aisha to prevent Granada from being extinct, leading to the well-known event when her son Boabdil gave the key of Granada to Isabella I of Castile and Ferdinand II of Aragon, the Catholic rulers of the fifteenth century. It is still unknown where Aisha truly stands in the annals of history, at the most pivotal moment in the history of Islam in Europe.

One of Aisha's most amazing qualities was her ability to compete in a male-dominated society. She was bold and assertive and not afraid to question the established quo. She questioned many of the prevalent ideas of her era, such as the notion that women were less valuable than men.

Her support of equality and justice is arguably Aisha's most potent legacy. She was a fearless defender of the weak and disenfranchised, speaking up against oppression and injustice wherever she witnessed it. One instance that highlights Aisha's commitment to equality and justice is when she spoke up for a group of women whose husbands were oppressing them. Justice for these ladies was aided by Aisha's lobbying and intervention on their behalf.

Legacy and Memory: Aisha in the History of Al-Andalus

Numerous historical analyses have been conducted on the kingdom of al-Andalus. The Iberian Peninsula was occupied to varying degrees by Arab monarchs and Muslim powers between 711 and 1492. Indeed, the cultural relevance and effect of nearly 800 years of non-Catholicism continue to impact today.

The Umayyad caliphate expanded eastward and westward at the beginning of the eighth century. The Visigoth ruling class was forced to flee northward due to their expansionist ambition, which took them to Northern Africa and, ultimately, across the Strait of Gibraltar to assault the Iberian Peninsula. Soon after, a Berber army under the command of generals from Damascus overran the majority of the region, dubbing it the caliphate "al-Andalus," with Seville as its capital.

But the fall of the Umayyad caliphate in 750 led to a change in leadership. The administration of Prince Abd al-Rahman I brought about a number of changes, including aspects of the Syrian politics and judiciary.

Al-Andalus would continue to be united, particularly in the tenth century, when the court of Cordoba became a haven for eminent thinkers, poets, and scientists. Eastern scientific knowledge and cultural exchange were advantageous to its residents. For centuries, Christians, Muslims, and Jews coexisted in an area controlled by the Arab elite, which contributed to the development of hybrid customs and ideas.

The Mozarabs, who were Iberian Christians living under Muslim authority and who assimilated Arabic culture and language, are a notable example of this, but there were challenges associated with this. Since doing so would elevate non-Muslims above Muslim citizens, they were prohibited from holding any management or administrative roles in the government. Male non-Muslims also paid an annual levy known as Jizya in exchange for their protected status as Muslims.

In the eleventh century, as the Umayyad Caliphate of Cordoba collapsed due to the civil war, several prominent Berber, Arab, and Muladí families seized the opportunity to establish their own separate kingdoms, known as Taifas. Meanwhile, the Christian kingdoms that occupied the northern portion of the Peninsula started to expand their dominion.

Certain Taifas established connections with the Northern African Almoravid and Almohad kingdoms in return for assistance against the Christians. However, this was insufficient to stop the numerous crusades and conflicts between the two factions, which were heavily impacted by the theological conflict and papal rhetoric. The final Nazari kingdom, Granada, collapsed in 1492.

Despite the vast historical span, al-Andalus' cultural legacies are still strongly felt in Spain today. Magnificent architectural structures were constructed, such as the Great Mosque of Cordoba and the Alhambra palace in Granada, which are priceless pieces of cultural heritage. However, perceptions of al-Andalus vary, as its historical influence has been both preserved and reinterpreted in different ways over the centuries.

Chapter Eleven

Rabia Balkhi: The First Persian Poetess

Poet Rabia Balkhi, also called Rabia al-Quzdari (or Khuzdari), wrote in Arabic and Persian in the tenth century. She is the first Persian-language poet known to be a woman. Originally a non-mystic poet, writers like Jami (died 1492) and Attar of Nishapur (died 1221) subsequently changed her imagery to that of a mystic poet.

Rabia's semi-legendary status is partly due to her romance with a slave named Bektash, which became a central element in the romanticised accounts of her life.

The Samanid Empire: Cultural Flourishing

The Samanid Empire's influence persisted from 819 until its decline in 999. In 875, the Samanid emir, Naṣr I, was granted the authority to rule all of Transoxania, establishing its dominance in northern Islam.

The Iranian renaissance finally materialised under the Samanid emirs, who succeeded the Ṭāhirid-Ṣaffārid rule in Khorāsān. The Persian language developed as a literary medium, deriving from the vernacular of northeast Iranian courts and homes and deftly utilising new Arabic terminology.

Pahlavi characters were finally dethroned in 697 when the brutal Umayyad administrator Ḥajjāj ibn Yūsuf ordered the switch to Arabic notation. Two centuries later, the Modern Persian's alphabet, derived from Arabic script, began to take shape as a written language. Poetry was the outcome of its discipline, which produced a very expressive and adaptable language with the flexibility that comes from flawless mastery of a very formal medium.

Because of the vivid imagery evoked by the lush landscapes depicted by Iranian poets—scenes that Arab poets of the desert were not familiar with—Arab prosody blossomed as a literary discipline. The Iranian epic tradition, exemplified by the fabled Shāh-nāmeh (Book of Kings), contributed to this cultural fabric. Ferdowsī of Ṭūs in Khorāsān spent three decades crafting this national epic, a masterwork of poetic narrative. The Samanid dynasty commissioned the work, which persisted after their downfall and was finished in 1009/10, preserving Iran's old stories and heroic mythology.

Bukhara competed with Baghdad as the Islamic cultural centre during the Samanid era. Patrons like Naṣr II (reigned 914–943) brought poets and scholars to Bukhara, and many of them produced literary and academic works in both Persian and Arabic. In addition to the Persian poet Rūdakī (died 940/941), who had crystallised the language and imagery of Persian lyrical poetry, as Ferdowsī (died between 1020 and 1026) was to do for that of the epic.

Following the Arab conquest, Iran flourished throughout the Samanid era. Saman-Khoda, a Zoroastrian who adapted Islam, established the dynasty in 819, and it was wholly Persian. The Samanids knew they were descended from the Parthians and the Sassanids. Although the Samanid kings and princes were wise, courteous, and loyal to the Abbasid Caliphs, they always tried to maintain their autonomy when ruling their realm. Furthermore, most of the Samanid court's ministers were well educated and literary individuals.

Because of his astute policies and fairness, Amir Ismail Samani increased the Samanids' power when he overthrew the Saffarids in

Khorasan in 900 CE. The nation saw positive development in terms of culture, art, commerce, science, politics, architecture, agriculture, and other areas. Bokhara, their capital, is a prime example of their astounding advancements in these fields.

Social security was high due to the government's stability, and there was a chance to improve everything. However, Ismail's successors could not continue as firmly as he did because they did not adhere to his policies. The first sparks of the Turk dynasties were ignited during the Samanid period, when the Iranian Turks were given unique places in the court. After 180 years of prosperous and magnificent rule, the Samanid dynasty was destroyed by the Karakhamids in 999.

Rabia's Poetry: Love, Loss, and Mysticism

Numerous historic monuments in northern Afghanistan have been destroyed, including the ancient city of Balkh, also referred to as the mother of cities. The shrine of Rabia Balkhi, the well-known poetess from a millennium ago, sits among the ruins. She was a recluse who spent her early years wandering around rural vineyards and penning motivational poems. There is mystery around the life of this young poetess. The ruler of Turan and Sajistan, Ka'b, was her father.

Her literary skills so impressed the residents of Balkh that they dubbed her a bird with golden wings. She had a deep appreciation for the beauty of nature and was particularly fond of her own country's gardens. She would go into a reflective state and compose her poetry while sitting next to the swift-moving brooks and streams of the gardens and orchards. Poetry has always been popular in Afghanistan, where four out of five people lack literacy, particularly among women.

Her own brother put her in jail when she fell in love with a slave. She encountered Baktash, a slave in Haris' court, one day while exploring the gardens of Haris, her older brother, who succeeded her father as monarch. As a sign of his love and friendship, the slave gave her a flower. She left the garden right away out of concern that someone may notice her. This tragedy fuelled her poetic career and ultimately resulted in her untimely death.

Her life was filled with the pains of love. From that point on, every line of her poetry was written with him in mind. She meditated about Baktash day and night while living in a dream world. Soon after, her brother heard about her romance and prevented her from meeting Baktash. She was unable to contain her emotions, so she wrote poems and gave them to the slave, who concealed them in a jewellery box. Baktah shared rooms with another slave, who one day opened the box in the hopes of discovering pricey diamonds.

He was surprised to discover only a few papers. After bringing the box to Haris, he examined the notes and discovered they were love letters from his sister to the slave. After receiving the messages, Haris grew enraged and gave the order to have his sister's veins cut and put into a boiling bath. The directives were executed. When the court attendants entered the bath after Rabia's death, they discovered what the desperate woman had scrawled in her own blood on the wall.

The Discovery of Rabia's Grave

Sometime in 1964, a burial site connected to Rabia Balkhi was found in the municipal park in Balkh. According to Tajik historian Akhror Mukhtarov (1924–2007), an "antiquarian" by the name of Sayyid Da'ud Agha and the khatīb (prayer leader) of the Khwaja Parsa mosque dug up the site.

The excavations were not conducted by any archaeologists with formal training. They discovered glazed tiles that they believed originated from Rabia's grave after excavating 1.5 meters below the surface. "No attention was paid to whether something lay beneath the tiles, or whether it was a tomb in fact, and if so, whether that of a man or a woman," writes Mukhtarov. But according to the majority of other accounts, it was a grave that was found.

It most likely originated from the premodern cemetery of the KhwajaParsa temple, which was levelled some thirty years ago to create the park's garden. Within a few years of its discovery, the precise method of its location appears to have been obscured by doubt. Elderly inhabitants claim that local officials found the grave in a dream or vision. Thus, Mukhatov's claim that the excavators were "assisted" by government authorities is important. Ghulam Rasul Paramach, a former Nuristani air force commander and the governor of Mazar-i Sharif, would have had local authority over the cemetery if it had been found prior to 1964.

He is undoubtedly the person most directly associated with the formalisation of the shrine. He was the official and journalist who visited Balkh's shrines and subsequently composed a poem in Rabi'a's own words. From the late 1950s until the early 1960s, he also held the position of director of culture and information for Balkh. The first book to popularise Rabia's story among the middle class in Afghanistan was his biography of her.

It contained excerpts from Nawabi's poetry and analyses by other Afghan academics, all of which contextualised the story within Afghanistan's historical geography. The book appeared in at least two editions, one before the grave's uncovering and one presumably released later. The formalisation of Rabi'a's shrine is more documented, although the circumstances surrounding the grave's finding are still unclear.

Rabia's Shrine through War and Development

The communist government and mujahidin organisations engaged in multiple battles over the town park of Balkh during the Soviet rule (1979–89). Even though the neighbouring monuments suffered significant damage, Rabia's shrine survived thanks to its reinforced concrete, despite being neglected and corroded. When the Taliban seized the northern parts of Balkh in 1998, the majority of the shrines, including

Rabi'a's, were shut down. However, after the Taliban were overthrown in 2002, shrine visits and the rituals and votive activities that went along with them quickly returned.

Rabia symbolises inspiration whose legacy addresses modern social challenges like arranged marriage, body autonomy, and street harassment. Over the past 20 years, there has been a steady increase in the belief that Rabia is a feminist icon.

Chapter Twelve

Sultanah Safiyya: Power and Politics in the Ottoman Empire

A singular event occurred during the Ottoman Empire's heyday that may have had a lasting impact on Eastern culture and global politics. During what is often referred to as "the Sultanate of Women," women gained influence.

Given that the Ottomans had stringent regulations to prevent such an event, this is remarkable for a number of reasons.

Even more remarkable is that the majority of these women, who showed remarkable leadership abilities, entered the court as slaves or concubines. Safiyya Sultana, who made a lasting impression on history in the late 16th and early 17th centuries, was one of the most amazing queens of that time.

The Ottoman Empire was influenced by her life story, political and diplomatic abilities, significant influence, and incredible capacity to forge strong alliances.

The Ottoman Harem: A Centre of Power

One of the most powerful and enduring kingdoms in world history was the Ottoman Empire. For 600 years, this Islamic-run superpower dominated major portions of the Middle East, Eastern Europe, and North Africa. The Sultan, the chief leader, was granted complete political and religious control over his subjects. Many historians consider the Ottoman Empire to have contributed much to regional security and stability, as well as significant advancements in the arts, sciences, religion, and culture, despite Western Europeans typically seeing them as a threat.

Osman Gazi (r. 1299–1324), the first ruler of the Ottoman dynasty and a Turkish tribal leader, is known in Italy as Ottomano, where the English word "Ottoman" comes from. He consolidated inherited and conquered territories under his control by using both force and diplomacy. His successors' victorious military expeditions expanded the empire eastward into the Caucasus and Anatolia, westward into Egypt and North Africa, and northward into the Balkans.

Ottoman sultan Mehmet II (who ruled from 1451 to 81) took control of the Byzantine capital, Constantinople (modern-day Istanbul), in 1453. The capital remained until 1923. The empire grew steadily in the 15th and 16th centuries, thanks largely to Mehmet II's leadership and legacy.

Despite numerous attempts to modernise and reform the army and civil institutions, the Ottoman Empire began to wane by the seventeenth century. By the eighteenth century, many of its lands in Europe, West Asia, and North Africa had disappeared. Mustafa Kemal Atatürk's contemporary Turkish Republic superseded the Ottoman state in 1923.

Curiosity has long surrounded the Harem of the Ottoman Empire. As the private residence of the Sultan's family, it held significant political influence. The harem's structure resembled a pyramid, with numerous groups and unique features at each level. A concubine, depending on her appearance, education, and surroundings, could be promoted to the position of princess-mother. High walls enclosed the entrance and were off-limits to all but males with certain responsibilities. When the presence of attractive concubines is taken into account, this institution became completely secret.

In Arabic, "harem" denotes "protected, holy and renowned thing or place." It is derived from the Arabic word h-r-m, which implies covering, disguise, disgusting, separating, and securing from others. Harem Eve is the term for the areas of homes, mansions, and palaces that are often designed to face the inner courtyard and where women can live comfortably without coming into contact with foreign men.

In the classical West, groups of Greeks and Romans lived in the back of houses, known as tugynaikeionded (women), and were separated from their men. According to a Sumerian tablet, the "women's house" where a barren woman was sent is most likely a harem. I Muawiya, the Umayyad Caliph, was the first to castrate attendants in the palace's harem area. Women's influence on state officials increased as a result of this process. This condition became apparent to the Abbasids, particularly in the early times.

While some of the women in the harem were well-known for their wealth, others were known for their involvement in official issues. Although there were no adequate records, it is known that the harem, where women and siblings resided among the Seljuks, had a special structure. The Seljuk sultans' harem consisted of concubines, servants, apartments, and infants.

The babies each had their own personalities, homes, and divans. Women were productive in the Seljuk government, just as in earlier eras. Under Sultan Mehmed II, the Conqueror of Constantinople, the Ottoman palace was established from the ground up and evolved as an institution following the state structure tradition.

QUEENS OF POWER

Harem has been a structure that offers training for women, and the state, court, and Enderun Sultan have used it to manage the service of men. Harem evolved into a sort of school that offers a multidisciplinary education based on knowledge, politeness, appropriate speech, and hard labour. In this regard, the harem's structure is comparable to a pyramid. Every layer has unique properties, and one's surroundings, education, and personal traits influence the capacity to transition between them.

Safiyya's Rise: From Captive to Sultanah

A singular occurrence occurred during the Ottoman Empire's heyday that may have impacted Eastern culture and global politics. During what is often referred to as "the Sultanate of Women," women gained influence. Given that the Ottomans had stringent regulations to prevent such an event, this is remarkable for a number of reasons. Even more remarkable is that the majority of these women, who showed remarkable leadership abilities, entered the court as slaves.

Safiyya Sultana, who made a lasting impression on history in the late 16th and early 17th centuries, was one of the most amazing queens of this time. In what is now Albania, Safiyya Sultana was born in 1550. Although she was originally from the Dukagjini Highlands, certain Ottoman court documents suggest that the Safiyya may have been born in Valona, which is now Vlora.

Safiyya was frequently mentioned in the chronicles and court records, regarded as primary sources. There is no room for question because the Queen's origin is mentioned numerous times in the diplomatic letters she exchanged and the reports from foreign embassies.

There are insufficient historical records to pinpoint the exact location of her birth. Her origins are frequently mistaken for those of her mother-in-law, who mistakenly believes Safiyya Sultan to be Venetian, or occasionally from Bosnia, who mistake her for her daughter-in-law.

Historians and academics agree that she was Albanian because of her ascent to power.

Safiyya is thought to have been fluent in several languages, including Albanian, which she was a native speaker of, which is further evidence of her ancestry. Little is known about her early life or family outside of her place of origin. As the Ottoman Empire extended its dominion over the Balkan region, Safiyya was born during a period of profound cultural and political change.

Despite being a volatile area because of the continuing battles at the time, Arbanon probably offered a rich and distinctive fusion of Western and Eastern cultural instruction because they were constantly at odds in the area. This might have signalled the beginning of Safiya's future rule and laid the groundwork for her extraordinary diplomatic abilities.

Even though Safiyya had modest origins, she was clearly more than just a peasant who happened to be extremely fortunate; she was educated, knew the procedure, and even had a keen sense of diplomacy and politics from an early age. In 1563, Safiyya Sultan visited the Ottoman court.

She was brought into the harem as a slave and given as a present to the future Murad III, the heir apparent to the throne. Because of her pale skin and golden hair, she was baptised there under the name Safiyya, which means "the pure one." Because there are so few historical records, it is difficult to determine whether she was taken as a slave or kidnapped during the conflict, or if she came from a wealthy family.

It is critical to keep in mind that throughout this period, Ottoman troops ravaged all of East and Southern Europe as well as the Balkans. Children and young adults, including those born into aristocracy, were frequently taken as slaves throughout the Ottoman Empire. Suleyman the Magnificent, who had 300 slaves in his harem, was in power when Safiyya arrived at the court. Harems represented both political and military might because the Ottoman Empire was fundamentally a theocracy and saw itself as a Muslim caliphate. The size of the sultan's harem increased as the Ottomans seized more territory.

Influence on the Empire: Safiyya's Political Maneuvering

Safiyya Sultan's public involvement in state politics was well-known. She also served as a significant advisor to Murad III and Mehmed III on government matters. She was able to boost her son's army patronage, but she also faced competition from other advisors, including viziers, the mufti, eunuchs, and other favourites.

The general public believed that Safiyya's meddling was excessive. Her unpopularity stemmed from the perception that she had overreached herself, surpassing the authority of the legitimate sultan. Additionally, she was perceived as overtly supporting Venetian interests.

In 1598, Safiyya, the ancestor of the other Ottoman sultans, started building the YeniValide Mosque in Istanbul, which Turhan Hatice eventually completed. In Cairo, the al-Malika Safiyya Mosque bears her name. Safiya also maintained cordial ties with England.

She convinced Mehmed III to allow the English ambassador to go to Hungary with him on a campaign. She personally wrote with Queen Elizabeth I of England, offering to petition the Sultan on Elizabeth's behalf, one distinctive feature of her career. Additionally, the two women traded gifts. Safiyya once obtained a portrait of Elizabeth in return for two silver cloth garments, one silver cloth girdle, [and] a pair of napkins wrought with massy gold.

The Legacy of Sultanah Safiyya in Ottoman History

Safiyya is regarded as one of the most influential sultanas in Ottoman history. She established an example for other women by using her authority like no other woman had. During the reigns of her husband, Murad III, and her son, Mehmed III, Safiyya stayed at the centre of the Ottoman court for over two decades.

One of Safiyya Sultana's strengths was managing international diplomacy. Throughout her political career, she maintained a very pro-Venetian stance, which greatly benefited bilateral relations and encouraged trade. Safiyya Sultana established frequent connections with Queen Elizabeth I of England even when her son was still a prince. She wrote the first letter suggesting a diplomatic partnership with the British king. The gold-sprinkled letter is currently housed in the British Museum.

Safiyya was well-known for her generosity. She donated a large portion of her fortune to help widows, orphans, and the impoverished. She also made significant donations to the Ottoman army. Several mosques, notably the well-known "Yeni Cami" (the new mosque) in Istanbul and the "Melike Safiyya Mosque," were constructed in her honour.

Queen Elizabeth highly valued Safiyya's position and abilities, seeing her as the British court's most potent ally in the Ottoman Empire. This facilitated signing several agreements, increased trade, and improved ties between England and the Ottomans. Other foreign embassies held Safiyya Sultana in the highest regard and regarded her as "a woman of her word."

Safiyya was undoubtedly among the women who obtained an excellent education during this period and were suitable for a future monarch. The all-powerful Mirhimah Sultana, the sole surviving child of Suleyman the Magnificent, is also thought to have strongly supported Safiyya and given her a great deal of political clout. Despite her aspirations, Mirhimah Sultana served as Safiyya's mentor, teaching her what she knew about internal diplomacy and how to handle the court's intrigues.

Chapter Thirteen

Queen of Sheba: Her Mighty Throne

Who was the Queen of Sheba? Was she the commander-in-chief of her rich and tranquil oasis and the sovereign leader of her state? Even if she worshipped the Sun God, was she the leader of the faithful? Or was she a kind of jinn, an apparition of a strong, independent woman who was terrible and deadly to rulers and patriarchy?

Nobody truly knows, although some claim the Queen of Sheba was a virgin marvel from Ethiopia, while others claim she was from Yemen and Southern Arabia. According to all reports, the Queen's grace, brilliance, knowledge, and leadership were universally admired.

King Solomon's (Sulaiman) and Queen of Sheba's Introduction

The story begins when King Solomon's threat to seize her paradise and usurp her Mighty Throne marks the culmination of the Queen of Sheba's narrative. A "warfaring man" and "a very good warrior who rarely paused from invading," Solomon was the world's ruler. Whenever he learnt of a monarch anywhere in the world, he would approach, degrade, and bring him under control.

To his surprise, Solomon promptly set out to subjugate this "last kingdom not yet within his control" after learning of the powerful Queen of Sheba. Armed with a letter, he dispatched his messenger/spy bird, the small hoopoe (hudhud), to the Queen and told it to wait for her response.

The three Abrahamic texts tell the tale of King Solomon's meeting with the Queen of Sheba, although none mention her by name. She is only referred to as Makida in the Kebra Nagast, the holy Ethiopian book of kings.

Her role as a sovereign queen—an autonomous woman with political power—identifies her as the Queen of Sheba. Whether from her mother, her father, or both, the stunning Bilqis (also known as the Queen of Sheba) acquired magical power and carried it in her blood. She was the daughter of a jinn mother (or father) and a human father (or mother).

When her father passed away, she was thirty years old, much past the traditional marriage age. She went on to become the Queen of Yemen after him. Infuriated by his actions and in response to the Yemenites' cries under this despot's control, Bilqis devised a bold plan. Despite the disapproval of his advisors, he gladly accepted her marriage proposal.

Once married, she planned to get him intoxicated: "severing his head and hanging it from the palace before sneaking away under cover of night is a symbolic act of removing his improperly overactive genitalia." The Yemenites celebrated her as their leader and saviour, applauding her liberating move. Bilqis became the undisputed ruler of Yemen and the Queen of Sheba, solidifying her position of power.

The Hoopoe's Message and the Queen's Strategic Response

The Queen of Sheba and King Solomon were initially unaware of one another. They become acquainted thanks to Solomon's spy/guide, a small hoopoe. The story begins with Solomon surveying his remarkable army, but he jumps into a rage after failing to spot the hoopoe amid the flock. He promises to kill the bird unless it has a valid reason or has its feathers pulled.

The hoopoe soon returns to Solomon's camp, and thankfully, he has a valid reason. The small bird informs its master that it has learnt something that the King is still unaware of. Solomon is subsequently told by the hoopoe about the Queen of Sheba, her affluent oasis, and how God has bestowed upon her a Mighty Throne, among other things. Perso-Islamic traditions claim that the hoopoe can sense water beneath the surface. It is said that this was why the King became enraged earlier—he needed water for his prayer ablution.

To a disbelieving Solomon and his army, the hoopoe explains that the Queen of Sheba and her supporters worship the sun because Satan (shaytan) has tricked them by keeping information about Allah (SWT) hidden from them. When the Queen asked her advisors what her ancestors worshipped, they replied, "They worshipped the Lord of Heaven," demonstrating her misguided faith. Since she couldn't see the god, she chose to kneel to the sun, believing nothing was more potent than its radiance.

The news deeply shakes the King. Did God not use the wind to keep him updated on all that occurred in his domain and beyond? Not quite! In "His" boundless wisdom, God wanted to occasionally humble Solomon and show him that his might had boundaries. Disbelieving, Solomon made the decision to verify the veracity of the bird's eyewitness report for himself. He handed the message to the hoopoe, telling it to deliver it to the Queen and watch for her response.

> *The message to the Queen was ominous: "Be ye not arrogant against me, but come to me in submission" (Quran 27:27–31)*

The Meeting and the Tests of Wisdom

The Queen was startled. She believed that a monarch must be "a mightier sovereign than herself" and that "any ruler who uses birds as his emissaries is indeed a great leader." The Queen was wise enough not to laugh at or disregard the threat posed by a strong foe. She carefully thought out her plan once more. They proclaimed their readiness to defend their leader, acknowledging her authority:

> *"We possess force and we possess great might. The affair rests with you; we follow your command" (Quran 27:32–33)*

However, the Queen of Sheba made the wise decision to give Solomon magnificent presents in the hopes that the gift-giving would act as a forerunner to a halt or avoid hostilities. The Queen of Sheba, who was equally bright as he was, chose to put him to the test to ascertain if he was a prophet or a monarch.

If he accepted her presents and gave her messengers a "look of wrath," the Queen reasoned, it would indicate that he was merely a king and not more powerful than she was; that his goal was political, and that he wanted to overthrow her and take away her powerful throne. However, it would indicate that he was a prophet of the Creator Allah (SWT) and would not be content until she bowed to him and adhered to his faith if he turned down her presents and seemed like a "friendly, amiable man."

Declaring that what God had given him was far more than what God had given her, Solomon turned down the Queen's gifts. Then he said that the Queen and her ambassadors were "a vainglorious people, attempting to surpass each other in things of this world" because they "did not know anything else," which is to say that they were only aware of power and greed. The Queen and her subjects were "abased and utterly humbled" when Solomon dispatched her ambassadors back with another menacing letter, warning of his impending attack and their deportation from their homeland.

The Queen of Sheba, convinced that Solomon was a divine prophet, decided to travel to Jerusalem to speak with Solomon to prevent her community's impending doom. Solomon, ever the strategic ruler, quickly seized power of her Mighty Throne. Upon seeing her throne in Solomon's possession, the Queen believed that he was not only a prophet but that she was no match for him, at least not militarily.

The wise queen then responded calmly, saying, "[It is] as though it were the very one," and that "we had submitted and we were given the knowledge beforehand." Solomon, having demonstrated his power, finally allowed the Queen of Sheba to enter his palace. But before granting her full access, he puts her through one final test.

Legacy and Interpretations of the Queen of Sheba

Both Sheba and Solomon possess a strong desire to learn more about one another. However, their approaches to joining forces result in different outcomes. The Queen sets off on a quest for knowledge after learning of the knowledge and justice of the prophet Solomon (Sulaiman). She hopes to unite "with one who has wisdom" through diplomacy, bridging, peacemaking, and perhaps even love.

In contrast, King Solomon seeks unity through force and appropriation, using his power to claim authority. After meeting with the Queen, Solomon sends her back to Yemen, where she retains her position in power, and visits her every few months.

Over time, the Queen of Sheba is reduced into an imaginary wife of the king, although one with certain caveats and ambiguity, by methodically removing her personality, autonomy, and authority. The queen's sexual subjugation and political defeat are celebrated by the patriarchal imagination, but her spiritual transformation and her autonomous acceptance of "the true faith (Islam)" are sadly lacking.

The Queen of Sheba was the temporal and spiritual head of her people. Her advisors and military commanders respected her authority and were prepared to fight for her. Although she was terrified, she was not intimidated by the prospect of battle, nor was she prepared to lead her people into a bloody fight. By adopting this stance, she might be seen as the ideal example of a compassionate and astute leader.

According to the Quran's revelations, she is neither a usurper ruler nor the daughter of a Jinn princess, and her sovereignty is not disapproved of by the general populace. Furthermore, God gave the sun-worshiping queen a Mighty Throne, which profoundly confused the sensibilities of Muslims in the Middle Ages.

At the conclusion of the story, King Solomon takes away the Queen of Sheba's Mighty Throne, sends her back to Yemen with a new spouse, and installs the new ruler and king of Yemen as the Queen's husband. Solomon then assigns jinn to look after the Queen of Sheba and serve her husband.

Chapter Fourteen

Conclusion

The narratives of remarkable Muslim female rulers throughout history reflect a tapestry of resilience, leadership, and vision. These women, bound by their circumstances yet empowered by their convictions, carved indelible marks on their societies, politics, and cultural landscapes. Their stories are not just tales of individual triumphs but also testaments to the extraordinary contributions women have made to Islamic empires and the world beyond.

Asiya bint Muzahim, the wife of Pharaoh, remains a timeless symbol of faith and defiance against tyranny. Her unwavering belief in the face of insurmountable oppression represents a spiritual and moral strength that transcends time. Asiya's story illustrates that power is not solely derived from worldly authority but also from a steadfast commitment to righteousness, even when it demands unimaginable sacrifice.

Razia Sultana, the only female ruler of the Delhi Sultanate, challenged entrenched societal norms and defied expectations. Her ascent to the throne was a groundbreaking moment in a patriarchal society, symbolising that competence and leadership are not confined to one gender. Despite the adversities she faced, Razia's legacy endures as a beacon of possibility for women in positions of power.

Sultanah Taj ul-Alam Safiatuddin Syah of Aceh exemplifies the resilience and strategic acumen that defined female leadership in Southeast Asia. Her reign stabilised Aceh and reinforced the region's significance as a center of Islamic scholarship and trade. Her contributions underscore the critical role of diplomacy and governance in ensuring prosperity and harmony.

The story of Nur Jahan, the influential empress of the Mughal Empire, is a testament to the power wielded behind the scenes. Her administrative skills and patronage of the arts left an indelible mark on the Mughal legacy. Nur Jahan's life reminds us that influence is not always overt but can shape empires in profound and lasting ways.

Shajar al-Durr's transformation from a slave to the Sultana of Egypt reflects the unpredictability of fate and the profound strength required to rise above one's origins. Her strategic mind and political acumen led to remarkable victories, including a pivotal role in repelling the Seventh Crusade. However, her tragic end serves as a poignant reminder of the volatility of power and the challenges women face in leadership.

In the Hausa states of Nigeria, Queen Amina of Zazzau symbolises military prowess and visionary leadership. Her campaigns expanded her kingdom's boundaries and secured its economic prosperity. Queen Amina's legacy is woven into the fabric of African history, embodying the duality of strength and compassion inherent in leadership.

Arwa al-Sulayhi, the Queen of Yemen, presided over a golden age of prosperity and cultural flourishing. Her administrative reforms and dedication to religious patronage demonstrated a nuanced understanding of governance. Arwa's reign is a powerful example of how leadership grounded in justice and inclusivity can leave a legacy that spans centuries.

Zaynab al-Nafzawiyyat's role as a powerful consort in the Almoravid Dynasty highlights women's multifaceted influence. Her strategic counsel and financial acumen fortified the empire's foundations, ensuring its longevity. Zaynab's story Emphasises that behind many great rulers lies a partner whose contributions are equally monumental.

QUEENS OF POWER

Queen Aisha al-Hurra of Granada represents the unyielding spirit of resistance during one of the most tumultuous periods in Islamic history. Her courage and leadership during the fall of Granada are emblematic of a deep-rooted sense of duty to her people and heritage. Even in the face of adversity, Aisha's resilience remains an enduring inspiration.

Rabia Balkhi, the first Persian poetess, offers a glimpse into the cultural and intellectual contributions of Muslim women. Her poignant poetry resonates with themes of love, loss, and spirituality, bridging the personal and universal. Rabia's life underscores the vital role of artistic expression in preserving and enriching cultural identity.

Sultanah Safiyya of the Ottoman Empire is a testament to the power dynamics within the imperial harem, a space often misunderstood and underestimated. Her political maneuvering and influence over the empire's affairs reveal the depth of agency women could exercise, even within constrained environments. Safiyya's story reminds us that leadership takes many forms and operates in varied arenas.

The enigmatic Queen of Sheba, whose story intertwines with that of Prophet Sulaiman (AS), embodies wisdom and diplomacy. Her journey to Solomon's court and the mutual exchange of knowledge exemplify the potential for cooperation and understanding between different cultures and kingdoms. Her legacy, rooted in religious and historical narratives, inspires discussions on leadership and intelligence.

Collectively, these women defied the constraints of their times, challenging stereotypes and reimagining the possibilities of female leadership within the Islamic world. Their lives demonstrate that the essence of power lies not merely in titles or conquests but in the ability to inspire, innovate, and lead with integrity.

The contributions of these queens, empresses, and leaders extend beyond their immediate realms, influencing generations and reshaping historical narratives. They navigated complex sociopolitical landscapes with courage, resilience, and wisdom, leaving legacies that continue to resonate. Their stories urge us to reexamine history through a lens that recognises and celebrates women's indispensable roles in shaping societies.

As we reflect on their achievements, we are reminded of the timeless relevance of their principles: justice, compassion, and the unwavering pursuit of progress. These values transcend borders and eras, guiding contemporary leadership and empowerment. The lives of these Muslim female rulers are not merely historical accounts but powerful reminders of the potential within us all to lead and inspire.

Through their stories, we find the courage to challenge injustices, the wisdom to navigate complexities, and the strength to rise above adversity. These women have paved paths that remain relevant in today's quest for equity and excellence. Their legacies, etched in the annals of history, inspire us to envision a world where leadership is defined by merit and vision rather than gender.

The echoes of their reigns call upon us to honour their contributions by fostering inclusivity, nurturing talent, and upholding the principles of justice and compassion. Their lives serve as a clarion call for all who dare to dream, lead, and transform the world around them. As we close this exploration of Muslim female rulers, their stories remain a beacon, guiding us toward a future where the potential of every individual is recognised, celebrated, and realised.

Find Out More

Website: www.barakahinbusiness.com

Socials: @barakahinbusiness

If you enjoyed this book, kindly leave a review to help expand our reach so others may benefit also.

www.ingramcontent.com/pod-product-compliance
Lightning Source LLC
Chambersburg PA
CBHW071218070526
44584CB00019B/3064